Storming Mont Albert By Tram

One Man's Attempt To Get Home

First performed aboard a W Class, #42 Mont Albert Tram
February 26 to June 6, 1982

Produced by TheatreWorks
Written by Paul Davies
Directed by Mark Shirrefs

Bringing the World
Back Together

A Picture Play

3rd Edition
Published by Gondwana Press, November 2019
Suffolk Park 2481 NSW

This book is copyright. Apart from any fair dealing for the purpose of private study, research or review, as permitted under the Copyright Act, no part may be reproduced by any process without written permission. Inquiries concerning publication, performance translation or recording rights should be addressed to the author.

Any performance or public reading of *Full House/No Vacancies* requires a licence from the author. The purchase of this book in no way gives the purchaser the right to perform the play in public, whether by means of a staged production or a reading.

© The moral right of the author has been asserted.

CONTENTS

Cast and Director   4

Storming Mont Albert By Tram

    ACT 1 (Inward Journey)   5
    ACT 2 (Outward Journey)   142

Critical Reception   249

Author   289

Dedication   291

Produced by

Directed by

Mark Shirrefs

With

Peter Sommerfeld
(Daniel O'Rourke)

Mary Sitarenos
(Alice Cronin)

Hannie Rayson
(Samantha Hart-Byrne)

Caz Howard
(Cathy Waterman)

Peter Finlay
(Nigel Davidson)

Tony Kishawi
(Terry Meagher)

Paul Davies
(Morris Stanley)

Graeme Stephen
(Snr. Const. Warren Wilkinson)
Brett Stewart
(Const. Cyril Foster)

* First published as a short story by Paul Davies, in The Journal (Dandenong-Springvale- Oakleigh) February 8, 1982.

STORMING MONT ALBERT BY TRAM

ACT ONE
(INWARD JOURNEY)

An audience gathers at the Mont Albert tram terminus (corner of Union and Whitehorse Roads) where they each buy a TravelCard:

And receive one travel sickness bag containing a programme.

Shortly after, at exactly 8.17pm (5.30pm Sundays) a green, W Class #42 Mont Albert tram arrives at the terminus from the city. The only people on board are a conductress, an irregular driver and an elderly, homeless man who appears to have passed out on a seat in the corner.

The connie, Alice Katranski, alights from the tram and goes to stop the traffic so her waiting passengers can safely cross and board.

On board, Daniel O'Rourke is sprawled out holding a transistor radio to his good ear while the other hand clutches the familiar bottle of 'cough syrup' wrapped up in colourful chemist's paper. He lives inside a dilapidated, filthy old leather coat with fading political badges from the late twentieth century stuck on it ("We want Gough!" and "Shame Fraser, Shame"). Understandably, other passengers (audience members) tend to avoid him as they come on - especially with the sound of his radio blaring through the tram. Finally though, some poor unfortunate has to squeeze in next to him because all 52 seats are soon filled.

Eventually the old drunk stirs in his sleep, lifts his head blearily and drops it onto the shoulder of the unfortunate person forced to sit next to him. Nearby passengers react as Danny's unlucky neighbour tries to lift the smelly old head up and away from them. Danny just mumbles in his sleep, reeking of alcohol. And drops his head over to the other side.

Towards the other end of the tram, as soon as everyone is settled, Alice surveys her passengers with obvious delight and introduces herself with a dizzy self-confidence.

> **ALICE**
> Hi, everyone! I'm Alice Cronin.
> I'm your connie for the evening
> and I just want to say, welcome aboard!

She looks around at them, smiling, tentative, a feather duster (which she uses to keep the tram spotless) tucked under one arm.

> **ALICE**
> (proudly)
> This is my first bit night solo.
> Working as a connie.
> Without a supervisor or anything...

She displays the bright red "P" plate stuck to the front of her uniform.

ALICE
...And I just wanted to say: if it all goes well, and I get a good report from the driver, they'll give me a permanent position...I'm so happy because this will be my first real job. Ever! So...Hey, I hope you all have a wonderful trip!

Still beaming at them, she goes to pull the cord to start the tram but is suddenly distracted by a fit of coughing which emanates from Danny's area down the back.

He clears some phlegm from a badly congested throat, looks around for a place to expectorate and is shocked to discover all these strangers suddenly gathered around him. So he swallows it and is soon snoring again.

Alice threads her way towards him.

>   **ALICE**
> Hey, mister, we're at the terminus now.

>   **DANNY**
>   (drowsily)
> Yeah.

>   **ALICE**
> Do you want to get off here?

His face drops forward and he snores on. She shakes him, tentative, gripping his shoulder with the old TAA airline bag slung over it.

>   **ALICE**
>   (louder)
> Excuse me... mister?

>   **DANNY**
>   (still barely awake)
> Yeah.
>   **ALICE**
> We're at Mont Albert now.

>   (she waits, nodding)
>   Where you paid to go. Dollar ten.
>   Time to get off.

Still no response. So Alice hits on a bright idea. Gently, she pulls the radio away from him and starts backing towards the door, eventually stepping down onto the street outside.

Danny seems to sort of sleep walk after her, dimly following the sound from his tranny.

>   **DANNY**
>   Hey, that's my tranny you've got there.
>   Hey...
>   Hey... Hey...

He follows her, erratically, to the footpath where she quickly places the transistor on a rubbish bin and races back to the tram, pulling the cord frantically, hoping to make a quick getaway.

Behind her, Danny scoops up his radio and shambles back on, just nudging ahead of Samantha Hart-Byrne who brings up the rear, signaling wildly, forced to jog the last few yards and nearly losing a high heel in the process.

                SAMANTHA
          (approaching from the footpath)
STOP! Oh Stop!
Please stop...

She manages to pull herself up on board, just as door closes and the tram takes off. Danny resumes his seat. Much to Alice's dismay.

                   SAM
            (breathless, to Alice)
Is this tram going to Melbourne, dear?

Alice takes the lighted cigarette out of Sam's expensive looking holder.

                   ALICE
I'm sorry, no smoking allowed on trams.

Alice takes a surreptitious puff herself before ashing it and dropping the butt in her bag.

                   SAM
   (disappointed about her smoke but offers no resistance)
Oh, but it *does* go down Collins Street?
                   ALICE
                  (brightly)
Sure does!

SAM
Do you know I've been waiting 25 minutes for a cab? It's absolutely impossible to hail one.

ALICE
(vaguely wishing she'd stop going on about it)
Mmmm.

SAM
I thought if I don't jump on this tram now I'll never get there. You know what the Melbourne Theatre Company is like.

Alice nods blankly. Not having a clue.

SAM
A few seconds late and you miss the entire first act.

ALICE
Well you're all right now.

SAM
Do I pay you or what?

ALICE
Just take a seat and I'll be with you in a minute.

Sam looks around at the unsavory lot occupying all the seats. She grimaces at the prospect.

SAM
(uncertain)
Sit anywhere?

ALICE
Sure.

SAM
But which end's first class?

ALICE
(proudly, gesturing around)
It's *ALL* first class.

SAM
Oh...

As Sam starts looking for a place to sit, she loses balance slightly, and accidently clumps onto Danny's foot. The weight of her stiletto explodes him back into life.

DANNY
(screaming in pain)
Ahhhhhhhh!!!!

He springs forward. Dropping his radio. Aghast.
Hopping on one foot.
Danny just hangs there, torn between shock, pain and anger. Staring down at his now silent tranny, trying to focus on what's actually happened.

DANNY
Ah No! Gawd, you've busted it.

He picks up his radio, shaking it and examining it closely.

SAM
I'm sorry about that.

Danny shakes it next to his ear, trying to get it to go. Then he rounds on her

DANNY
Fifteen quid on "General Strike" in the last at Monee Valley and I won't even be able to hear the race!

He staggers back into his seat suddenly aware of the shooting pain in his left foot.

DANNY
(tugging at the shoe, balancing on one leg)

16
Gawd, what have ya done down here?

SAM
Look - I lost balance, I'm not used to trams...
Please don't take that off.
(pressing her scarf against her nose)

Too late. He takes off a shoe and then the rubber glove which he has been using as a 'sock' (the tips of the 'fingers' have been cut off to fit his toes through). He hands the glove to Sam, she recoils in horror. It glistens with his sweat and toe jam.

DANNY
Here, hold that for me, would you love?

He indicates his glistening rubber 'sock'.

DANNY
(explaining to those around him)
Well, I've got to keep me foot dry haven't I !?

Sam looks suddenly anxious, bending around to glance out through a window.

> **SAM**
> (agitated)
> Has anyone seen a Mercedes going past?

> **DANNY**
> She's definitely broken something.
> (examining his filthy toes)
> There's no feeling in the little cashew.

> **SAM**
> Sorry to have disturbed your sleep, alright?

> **DANNY**
> Sleep!?
> Lady, I don't sleep. I think.

> **SAM**
> (sarcastic)
> Yes, I suppose you do.

> **DANNY**
> I think while you sleep.

> **SAM**
> How astonishing.

> **DANNY**
> (savours the idea, reconsiders)
> I think, *because* you sleep.

Much to Sam's relief, Alice at last comes back to collect her fare.

> **SAM**
> (smiling)
> How much is it to Melbourne, dear?

                    ALICE
                (smiling back)
A dollar, ten thanks.
                    SAM
                (shocked)
A dollar, ten!
            (rummaging through her purse)
My god! I hope you don't expect a tip!

Sam is joking but Alice's smile falters a little.
Behind Sam, Danny is peeking into her open purse.
Assessing his chances.

                    SAM
Do you take Visa?
                    ALICE
Nope.
                    SAM
Mastercard?
                    ALICE
Nope.
                    SAM
Amex?
                    ALICE
Nope.
                    SAM
Do you take Myer's?
                    ALICE
We don't take cards.

                    DANNY
                (holding out his tranny)
Don't expect you can solve this by throwing money at it either.

                    SAM
                (huffy)
I have no intention to.

Sam hands Alice a fifty dollar note. Alice sighs at the change this will take, but clicks a ticket and hands it back to her. With all the change.

SAM
(putting the ticket and money back
in her purse, clicking it shut)
Thank you very much.

DANNY
Well I'm not asking.

SAM
And I'm not offering.

DANNY
(thinking hard)
Good.

SAM
Good.

DANNY
Good.

SAM
(back to Alice)
You haven't seen a Mercedes going past have you, dear?

ALICE
No.

Danny experiences another sudden stab of pain from his foot, starts rubbing it.

DANNY
Christ, I thought they were nailing me to the bloody cross.

But Sam remains distracted, constantly looking out at the traffic going past. Hoping to spot a particular Mercedes.

> **DANNY**
> But it's alright, lady- don't you worry, I won't say another thing about it.

> **SAM**
> That's the first good news I've had all night.

Danny struggles to put his 'sock' and shoe back on.

> **DANNY**
> It's the victim who pays the price. While the rich get away with it.

> **SAM**
> (back to Alice)
> Is it always this crowded, dear? I mean, do I have to stand all the way to Melbourne?

> **ALICE**
> I'm sure some gentleman will ... (stand up for you)...

> **DANNY**
> No one will stand up for ya love. Not these days.
> (lifts his arm to mime holding a strap)
> Afraid of 'BO'.
> No there's no manners left in the world.
> No sense of caring and sharing.
> But you can have my seat, alright?
> (struggles to his feet again, crossing in front of her)
> Just park it in there...

Sam hesitates, then takes out a small bottle of 4711 perfume spraying Danny's seat and taking off her scarf to wipe it thoroughly, before settling into it.

He hovers above her now, positions reversed, looming down with only his bad breath standing between them.

DANNY
Happy now?

Sam turns to look out the window. Trying to ignore him. Hoping he'll go away.

Alice is still there. Hanging nearby, waiting to assert her authority.

ALICE
(to Danny)

Fares thanks.

Danny just ignores her. Swings around, addressing the rest of the tram.

DANNY
No- I usta stand up and be counted once. Once, in 1970 they arrested so many of us moratorium marchers we had to be taken up to Russell Street and tried in a prosecutor's office out the back!
(still snickers at the memory of it)
"Where's the evidence that this is a courtroom," I said, "your honour, eh?"

ALICE
(persisting)

Fares thanks.

DANNY
(rounding on her as if she's the magistrate)
"And where's the evidence that you're even a magistrate?" I pointed out cleverly. He said, "I don't have to prove to you that that I'm a magistrate." "Well, then," I said "how do I know you just didn't walk in here off the street! After all...

ALICE & DANNY
(she joins in - together:)
...this courtroom looks more like a broom cupboard!"

Danny scrutinizes her - wondering how she knew the line.

ALICE
You told that joke on the way out.

Danny throws back his head and laughs again at the memory of it.

DANNY
Gawd, those were the days, eh?...Bourke Street packed solid...Jim Cairns leading the way...you felt like you had a hundred thousand friends. Yep, voted with me feet in the street, I did - or with what's left of 'em. Poor crushed things. Wouldn't credit I used to tutor in anthropology would you? All my Monash students ended up in Nimbin at the Aquarius festival. Turned into hippies.
(still underwhelmed by the fact)
And now, here I am... just another leftover radical activist.

Alice is becoming more insistent.

ALICE
Fares thanks.

Danny looks at her as if noticing her for the first time. Then frowns, sobers a little, starts searching in his pockets. Firmly back in the present again.

DANNY
Ah- home, thanks, love.

ALICE
(fatalistically)
And where's that, as if I can't guess?

DANNY
Mont Albert, love, thanks. That's where I'm goin'... Down a little lane to the thousand star hotel. Just behind Beckett park.

Danny is rummaging in his many pockets for coins, starts counting them into her hand. Small denominations, mostly copper.

ALICE
(firmly)
We've just left Mont Albert.

Danny blinks at her, looks blank for a moment, then suddenly swings and peers out a window.

DANNY
What time is it?

ALICE
(checking her watch)
It's twenty-five past eight.

He frowns, thinking hard.

>   DANNY
> Would that be, like ... you know ...twenty five past eight in the morning or twenty five past eight in the afternoon?

>   ALICE
>   (losing patience, throwing up her arms)
> What's it look like?!

>   DANNY
> I dunno, it's this daylight saving, love, mucks it all up, it's got me beat.

>   ALICE
> Look, I've gotta take your fare, alright?

>   DANNY
> Alright! Well how much is it to Mont Albert?

>   ALICE
>   (voice rising)
> We've just left Mont Albert!!

                    DANNY
    Well, I'd like to go back!

Alice tries another tack, produces a transport map of
Melbourne and shows him a Travelcard.

                    ALICE
    Look! You buy one of these, see?
                (indicating the card)
    Then you can sleep on public transport all over
    Melbourne
                    DANNY
                (looking blankly at the card)
    One of them?

                    ALICE
    A section one travelcard. Section One, right?
      (showing him where Section One is on the map)
    See the yellow bits?
            (counting the numbers on her fingers)
    It's the new ticketing system. It's really quite simple -
    well almost.
    Now there are 1,2,3,4,5,6,7,8,9,10 different travel
    cards.
    Now number one is $1.10. It's called 'Central'. 'Central'
    is for the central area.
        (rattling it all off at an increasingly frantic pace)
    Then the number two is really the number one plus
    another zone and another dollar. So that includes the
    central zone plus zone one, which is this area where
    we are now. Or are about to go out of.
                (indicating it on the map)
    So if you're going to the city you will need to get travel
    card one plus two, not this one and two, but finger
    four.
     (holding up four fingers, and losing the plot a little)

ALICE (cont)
You see, out of the ten different fingers - I mean travel cards - with a one/two card you can travel in zones 1 and 2 and that includes to the city and back, including Mont Albert for as long as you like, until the day is over. At midnight. Whichever comes first. Simple. Therefore it's a finger two travel card. That's a dollar ten, please.

Danny turns from her jutting fingers to the other passengers.

DANNY
Isn't she a good lass bothering to explain all that to me.

ALICE
(indicating the travel map)
Didn't you get one of these in your letter box.

DANNY
(coy)
Well, ah, I don't have a letter box, love, you see, right at this moment. I'm sorta between residences as a matter of fact.

ALICE
(holding up a travelcard)
Well, if you want to travel on this tram all night you've got to have one of these.

DANNY
(rummaging in his pockets again)
But I got a ticket.
(finds it, shows it)
I got a ticket off you before.

ALICE
That's what I'm *saying*. It wasn't a travelcard. It was a two hour ticket. It only lasts two hours and takes you one way.

DANNY
I only want to go one way - home!

ALICE
So now you've got to get another one.

Danny looks at the map, looks at Alice, makes a despairing gesture. It's all too complicated.

Meanwhile the tram stops and Cathy Waterman gets on. She moves down the front of the tram where she starts putting on a bit of makeup, checking the results in a small mirror.

Alice rings the cord twice to start the tram and turns back to Danny. He anticipates another harangue.

DANNY
(appealing for mercy)
I can't understand it, love. The coloured bits. It's all the colours, you see...in my state of health - and I am in fragile health, you know. But I'm SORRY but you're just going to have to go through it once more, you know.
(apologetic, rising to panic)
Because, really, I just want to GO BACK TO MONT ALBERT!!!

ALICE
(calmly, clearly, simply)
We can't go back.

DANNY
(alarmed)
Why not?

ALICE
Because this is a tram.

DANNY
But I want to go back.

ALICE
But you can't go back.

DANNY
I want to go back.

ALICE
You can't go back.

DANNY
But I want to!

ALICE
But you can't!

DANNY
WHY NOT!!!

ALICE
(finally losing it)
BECAUSE THIS IS A TRAM!!!
IT DOESN'T *GO* BACKWARDS!!!

Danny settles a moment. Letting it sink in.

DANNY
Then how come it was going backwards on the way out?
(pointing to the rear driver's box)

Alice gives up, she pulls the cord to stop the tram.
Danny can see what's coming.

DANNY
Look, love...

ALICE
You're getting off.

SAM
(listening in from nearby)
Here here.

Alice walks away from him. Dismissing him already. He follows, humble.

DANNY
Look, love, I just want to go where...
(from pleading to a rising sense of injustice)
I paid to go, you know!!

ALICE
And I really want you to go there too.

SAM
I think we all do.

ALICE
(rounding on him, fed up)
Look, you wanna go back to Mont Albert...
So you get off at the next stop, right?
You walk across the road to the stop on the other side.
(indicating)
Then you get the - next - tram - back - to - the - terminus.

And she goes down the front end of the tram to collect Cathy's fare.
Leaving Danny just hanging there.

DANNY
(to nobody in particular)
What next tram?
I don't see any trams.
How do I know there IS another tram, eh?
(calling after Alice as she gets further away
and he grows more confidant)
Hey, miss!

DANNY
Where's the evidence that THIS isn't the next tram to Mont Albert?
(laughs)
Looks more like a Sydney ferry to me.

As Alice comes up to Cathy:

CATHY
(holding out two dollars)
'Pensioner concession thanks.

Alice barely hides her shock. This woman is pensioner ? She takes in Cathy's make-up and shiny, thigh hugging tights, the skimpy black chemise, the extraordinarily high heels.

ALICE
(dubious)
One pensioner concession...

Alice smiles lamely, her disbelief quite evident. But she takes Cathy's two dollars, clips a ticket nevertheless, and hands it to her with a dollar twenty change.

At the same time, down the other (back) end of the tram, Danny is on his soapbox again. Muttering to no one in particular - whoever he can lock eyes with.

DANNY
Should be free anyway - public transport. Save the petrol!
(winks at someone)
I reckon.

                    DANNY (cont.)
Never add up the real cost of cars, do they? Eh?
                    (he relaxes into it)
When they close another rail line they never add up
the cost of all the trucks and bridges and lead
poisoning that replaces it, do they? All the car
insurance and road trauma. No. NO, they never put
that in the debit column when they say the trams are
losing money. Gawd, it's ridiculous, it's absolutely,
utterly unconschunable - consch - unable,
unconscionable...
                    (fumbling his words)

By now the tram has stopped from Alice's cord-pull,
but Danny remains on board.

Samantha Hart-Byrne takes the opportunity to move
towards Alice who remains up the front of the vehicle.
Away from Danny and close to the driver.

                    SAM
                    (to Alice)
Doesn't look like he's going.

                    ALICE
                    (resigned)
Ah well -.

                    SAM
Yes, but don't you think you should do something?

                    ALICE
                    (shocked)
Do something?
                    (like what?)

                    SAM
Well, yes, I think you should tell the driver.

ALICE
The driver? Tran? Oh yeah, he already knows. They had a punch-up on the way out.

Sam looks shocked and disgusted.

While down the back, Danny continues to harangue anyone who will listen.

DANNY
Take us all here, eh? The car-less society. Car-free kids too young to drive, old coots like me, too smart. And all the rest of you.
(sweeping his arm around unsteadily)
Who can't afford it. Well, I tell ya what: 'General Strike' in the last at Monee Valley...
(winks, nudges someone)
Put ya pension cheque on him and you'll be laughing
(laughs)

Danny stops abruptly, struck by another sudden, depressing thought, he rummages in his many pockets again for a form guide.

DANNY
Or was that yesterday? Oh Geeze, wait a minute...

Sam can't believe there's nothing to be done about him.

                    SAM
              (back to Alice)
I mean, we pay enough in taxes for a decent social welfare system - well, I don't personally, Michael and I have reduced our tax burden to basically zero... But some people pay a lot and it's just not fair. You'd think that with all the money they collect there'd be some place he could be taken care of? A home or something?

                    ALICE
I don't think he'd go.
              (shrugs)
Anyway, he's harmless enough.

Sam can't quite accept Alice's flippant attitude, she glances back at Danny a few times and tries again.
                    SAM
Well, I'm sorry but he's really getting on my nerves. It's not right that people should be subjected to it.

                    ALICE
              (vague, non-committal)
Mmm...

SAM
I mean, the worst thing you can do is to give them money. What they really need of course is a decent meal. But you buy them a pie or a Big Mac and what happens after that you wonder?

ALICE
Mmm...

Danny has finally located the racing form, in one of his pockets and un-crumbles it.

DANNY
(squinting at the page with his good eye)
Christ no! 'General Strike' was the double with 'Acidity' at Flemington. Ah- what! I don't believe it! My bloody memory...
It's Friday

DANNY
(he's a couple of days out)
Geezus, Friday already. I've bloody missed the race. Shit!

Finally Sam can stand it no longer. She snaps and rounds on Danny with a sudden manic shout.

SAM
Oh will you SHUT-UP!

DANNY
(yelling straight back)
There's definitely something not in working order down there.
(indicating his bruised foot)

Sam turns back to Alice as if that last exchange with Danny just didn't happen. He mumbles on in the background.

SAM
I know the unemployment situation is rather fluid, I mean, I tried to get a job with a BA from La Trobe but all I could manage was a part-time position scanning telemovies to work out where the ads should go. Now, whenever things reach an emotional climax with Michael I half expect a commercial break to occur....

DANNY
(firing back)
Get off and wait for another tram!
As if that's all I've got to do all day!
Wait for trams

Finally Sam snaps

SAM
WILL YOU JUST SHUT UP YOU PARASITE!
(back to Alice, starting to break down)
And now he's gone and dumped me.

ALICE
Who?

SAM
(annoyed that she isn't keeping up)
Michael! When I said "Stop the car" I never expected him to *let* me get out, let alone *drive off* and *leave* me there. It was a figure of speech.

ALICE
Oh... so he left you on the...at the terminus...

SAM
Dumped me on the footpath like so much...rubbish. As if there's nothing more to say after five years of marriage, but "get out and good riddance!" It's almost as bad as some tawdry soap opera.

Alice, looking for an excuse to extricate herself from this emotional whirlpool, notices Danny attempting to reach for the cord.

                    ALICE
          Looks like he's going at last...

And she moves away from Sam towards the back of the tram.
Sam tries to compose herself, taking out a small make-up case with mirror and eyeliner and is soon caught up in her own reflection, making tiny facial adjustments.

Alice pulls the cord for Danny as she approaches him.

                    ALICE
            (conversational, glad that he's going)
          How you feeling now?

                    DANNY
          I'm not, love, I'm not feeling at all.
          I'm mainly relying on hearing and eyesight.

The tram stops and Nigel Davidson gets on. He hangs around the centre of the tram, holding a videotape container and briefcase, Nigel wears sunglasses and a "Solidarity" t-shirt (from the Polish anti-communist trade union movement of the early 1980s). He looks like someone trying very hard to appear straight while still a bit out of it. He puts the video under one arm then drops it as he reaches for a hand rail with the same arm. Clearly not quite getting it together.

The tram remains stationary.
                    ALICE
              (prompting Danny)
          You want to get off here?
                    (hopefully)

                                DANNY
How can I get off if I can't even walk!?

Alice pulls the cord twice to start the tram again.

                                ALICE
Alright, but you're only getting further away from where you said you wanted to go.

                                DANNY
That's true of the whole world, love.
Yeah, that's the trouble.

Alice moves off to get Nigel's ticket. As she comes up:

                                NIGEL
City thanks.

Alice gives him a ticket. He gives her a ten dollar note wrapped around the flower from his button hole. She reacts. Smiles, takes note and flower. It's the sort of thing that reminds Alice that her job isn't totally one of pushing manure uphill. She puts the flower in the top pocket of her uniform. Nigel likes the effect. Smiles, winks at her, takes his ticket and his change. Clearly a ladies man.

                    NIGEL
                (fetching smile)

    Thanks.

He remains standing, but leans back in one corner of the tram's small entry foyer as Alice starts writing figures in her book: the numbers of the various types of tickets sold so far.

Samantha has been chewing over the last few minutes, and probably over the last few years of her life. She passes Nigel as she plows on towards Alice again, the only sympathetic ear available.

                    SAM
    I just wanted you to know I'm not utterly dependent on Michael.

Alice looks up from her calculations, slightly perplexed.

> **SAM**
> I've always prided myself on that.
> I've never been utterly dependent on anyone.

Alice is not quite sure what to say, but not wanting her to break down again.

> **ALICE**
> Oh good.

> **SAM**
> He even accused me once of being trendy.

> **ALICE**
> (sympathetic)
> Ah...

> **DANNY**
> That must've been a long time ago, love.

Sam stabs a venomous look at him, but chooses to ignore the remark.

> **SAM**
> You know, my dear, I am *not,* repeat *not,* trendy. I loathe trendy people. I mean, all the trendies left our gym ages ago.

> **ALICE**
> Oh...

> **SAM**
> Because of course, when you're married to Michael, you're not supposed to *do* anything. I can't abide charity work, I'm bored stiff with shopping, so I'm supposed to sit at home and co-ordinate the housekeeping.

ALICE
Why don't you tell him how you feel?

SAM
Oh I intend to, I intend to make it all very painfully clear. The next time he tells me to throw a dinner party I'm going to throw one, alright. I'm going to throw it all over him!

Alice is amused.

SAM
And I will, too. I'm not joking.
I mean he expects me to be perfect. The perfect wife, the perfect cook, the perfect hostess, and oh yes, his mother can do it, but she's got *Help*!
I don't of course, I don't have *Help*! Michael thinks that's just too "bourgeois". Just because he had to do everything for himself in boarding school. I told him in the car just now, I said "Michael, I need *HELP!*

DANNY
That's an understatement.

They ignore him, Alice quickly covering...

ALICE
And he didn't accept that?

SAM
He laughed. He tossed back his Terence Marini hairdo and laughed. He said "You've got Mrs. White to do the ironing, what more do you want? I saw then just how *ugly* he was. I mean, he even threw Cynthia Monstephen up as some kind of example.

DANNY
I'd regurgitate her meself.

In the centre of the tram Nigel has slipped a small camera out of his briefcase and is quietly snapping away at different people in the tram, trying to catch them when they're not looking. Part of a documentary composed mostly of stills which he'll try and put together when his current script development funding runs out. Then catching his own reflection in the glass door, finds he can't resist taking selfies.

But Sam notices none of this. Too caught up in her own drama.

SAM
It's pathetic really. Cynthia's so trivial she even went on *Sale of the Century.*

ALICE
Oh - did she win anything?

SAM
The Franco Cozzo furniture. I can see it fitting in perfectly with their Surfers' penthouse. She's *so* Beaumaris kitsch! Pathetic really. It proves my point that new money has nothing but a bad effect on people. You've only got to look at Michael. I thought I'd rather get in a cab than travel another inch with him. It was simply continue under my own steam or a slow suicide back home in front of the *Don Lane Show.* Naturally I chose the theatre.

                    ALICE
Naturally.

And Alice continues cleaning the tram with her feather duster. Suddenly, down the other end, Nigel has swung away from his own good looks and spotted Cathy through his viewfinder. Both his jaw and his camera drop in unison, his heart skips a beat as he lifts his sunglasses to get a better look. Tentatively, pulse racing, he edges towards her. It takes a moment for Cathy to recognize him. And immediately remains nonplussed.

                    NIGEL
Cathy? Cathy Waterman?
                    CATHY
            (underwhelmed/resigned)
Hullo Nigel.
                    NIGEL
Hey, how are you?
                    CATHY
I'm...okay...better...

NIGEL
You look pretty good.

CATHY
(matter of fact)
Yeah, I'm alright. My neck still gives me a bit of trouble.
(rubbing it)

NIGEL
Your neck?
(puzzled)
Your neck is still giving you trouble?

CATHY
Yeah, so how are you.

NIGEL
Your neck? You're saying, that time I threw the...

CATHY
(impatient)
Yes, it still hurts.
(running on, nonchalant)
How are you?

NIGEL
I'm fine...you know... surviving...

CATHY
I heard you ended up in Sydney.

NIGEL
Yeah.

CATHY
It's been quite a while.

NIGEL
Yeah. Too long.

CATHY
But time wounds all heels, eh Nigel?

NIGEL
(taken aback)
What? Are you kidding? After six years - I'm still a... You're still bitter? A heel?

CATHY
What an amazing coincidence.
(doesn't sound like it)

NIGEL
Yeah amazing.
(nodding, slight pause)
Are you... what, living out here or something? Still living in Melbourne?

CATHY
Deepdene, actually.

NIGEL
Deepdene!
(trying to make a joke of it)
You're not dropping out of the human race are you?

NIGEL/CATHY
(together)
"Depends what you mean by human."

Obviously an old joke they share.

CATHY
You haven't changed much.

NIGEL
(seriously)
I've changed a lot, Cathy.

CATHY
(dubious)
Oh yeah?

NIGEL
'Shouldn't judge a film by its subtitles.

CATHY
So your biro broke down did it?

NIGEL
What?

CATHY
I never got any letters.

NIGEL
I gave up putting my feelings on paper.

CATHY
Yeah. I heard you'd been ruining a couple of films.

NIGEL
Tapes. I'm a tapemaker now. I do clips for a couple of Sydney bands. That's why I'm down here, we're scouting locations for a new LP.

CATHY
What sort of bands?

NIGEL
"The Bad Tempers"

CATHY
Who?

NIGEL
"Delusions of Grandeur"

CATHY
The name of your company?

NIGEL
They're a born-again, reggae outfit.

CATHY
Oh-

NIGEL
The "Tempers" are strictly punk.

CATHY
You make a living out of that?

NIGEL
It's better than doing ads. I've still got integrity.

CATHY
Sounds like you've finally made it.

NIGEL
(modest, dismissive)
Nah - But yeah...I suppose...

CATHY
Your career just took off didn't it?

NIGEL
You mean my North Korea or my South Korea?
(bad joke, didn't work)

CATHY
I mean your life long self-promotion exercise.

But Nigel remains bemused, just hangs there grinning, shaking his head.
Still the same old Cathy.

NIGEL
(almost accusative)
But why bury yourself in Bogansville?
What happened to North Fitzroy?

CATHY
I felt like having a backyard.

NIGEL
(disbelief, slight digust)
A backyard?

CATHY
Maybe I couldn't handle the smog.

NIGEL
But it's the *suburbs* forgodsake.
(distastefully)
I mean, *Melbourne suburbs*. Dogs' poo and hideous shopping centres. People in motorised wheelchairs with shorts and long sox.

CATHY
(defensive)
I like dogs and shopping centres. And now you're being ageist. You could end up in a motorized wheelchair too.

NIGEL
(unconvinced)
Oh yeah?

CATHY
At least in Melbourne people think.

NIGEL
No. They only *think* they think.

CATHY
Look, Nigel, I know Sydney, it's all form and no content, I can see why it suits you.

NIGEL
Sixty percent of people living in Melbourne actively wish they were somewhere else.

Cathy sighs audibly.

NIGEL
You realize what that says about the place?

CATHY
So I like being in a minority.

NIGEL
(driving it home)
Sixty percent.

CATHY
God! You're so- Sydney-centric.

NIGEL
The only time I hear about Sydney is when I come to Melbourne.

CATHY
Well what are you doing out here in the suburbs if you're so cynical about the place?

NIGEL
' Drummer friend of mine's got this handy little greenhouse in East Kew.

He takes out an elaborate cigarette case, offers her a pre-rolled smoke.

NIGEL
Like to try one?

CATHY
(wishing he would just disappear)
No!

NIGEL
Drummer's grow the best stuff.

Cathy is acutely aware of people around them, overhearing this.

CATHY
(warning)
Nigel -

NIGEL
(still holding out the cigarette case)
Go on.

                      CATHY
I like reality the way it is.

                      NIGEL
Ah- reality's a drag.

He puts the case away.

                      NIGEL
Get it?

                      CATHY
What?

                      NIGEL
        (mimes a taking a toke, grins)
A drag.

                      CATHY
        (groans)
Oh god! Are you stoned already?

While this has been happening, Danny has been fiddling down the back with his tranny again, shaking it, trying to will it back to life. Eventually he gives up. Refocuses his attention onto Samantha.

> **DANNY**
> You wouldn't have the time would you love?

She completely ignores him.

> **DANNY**
> Excuse me, love...

> **SAM**
> I don't have a watch!

> **DANNY**
> Perhaps I could interest you in one...

He rolls up his sleeve, exposing an armful of dodgey watches.

> **DANNY**
> Men's, ladies, digital...

> **SAM**
> No thank you.

> **DANNY**
> Solar powered?

> **SAM**
> I said NO!

> **DANNY**
> Fully guaranteed.

> **SAM**
> Will you please go away!

So Danny turns to another passenger. Showing his arm.

                    DANNY
    How about ten quid for the black one, mate?
    It was going only yesterday.
            (shakes it, holds it up to his ear)

But the passenger clearly isn't buying.

                    DANNY
    Well what would you say to a transistor radio? Works fine.
             (switching it on, nothing happens)
    Made in Japan. You know...just that on the tram all the wires make the reception a bit statick-y. Works fine, though. Had it on earlier this evening... No?

So he goes for another unlucky passenger.

DANNY
Excuse me... excuse me do you have the time at all, mate?

Perhaps this passenger does have a watch and tells Danny the time, so he tries another person, working his way around the back of the tram.

While up the front, Nigel makes another attempt to engage Cathy.

NIGEL
Anyway, you never wrote to me.

CATHY
(still angry about it)
I didn't know where you'd gone for twelve months!

She becomes aware of how loud she's sounding, strangers listening in.
So she moderates a little...

CATHY
Can we talk about this another time?

NIGEL
I needed a change, Cathy. I really did.

CATHY
(still bitter)
Yeah, well, so did I.

NIGEL
I know, I know... So I split, didn't I?
I wanted to give you a chance to work it out.

CATHY
Yeah, well, I've had six years to sort it out, Nigel.

Again she goes to distance herself from him. He follows slightly. Guilty slightly, but persistent certainly.

NIGEL
Look, I admit I behaved badly, you know. Point taken. But you got to admit you were blocking, Cathy, you were really brick-walling back there in Scotchmer Street.

CATHY
Is that your account of it? After six years? I was 'blocking'!?
Where'd you pick that up, some holistic clinic or something?

NIGEL
There was this correspondence course in Group Therapy.

CATHY
Grope therapy - more like it.

Again she makes to move away from him. Again he follows.

NIGEL
You don't believe I've changed do you?

CATHY
I can see your eyes are more bloodshot.

NIGEL
(whispering)
Confidentially, Cathy, I've been undergoing analysis.

CATHY
(out loud)
Finally you had to pay someone to listen to you.

NIGEL
(a little hurt by that)
Hey, come on, it's been good for me. I've modified. I'm a different person.

CATHY
(dubious)
Oh sure-

NIGEL
In fact, I'm...planning to terminate.
In about twelve months I should be pretty well...

CATHY
Cured?

NIGEL
Emotionally secure.

CATHY
Twelve months? To find out if your neurosis is real or just a figment of your imagination?

NIGEL
You can't go cold turkey from a shrink, you know.

CATHY
Did he tell you that?

NIGEL
(again the whisper)
I've learned how to yell, Cathy.

CATHY
(groaning audibly)
Nigel. Please don't do anything embarrassing.

NIGEL
The breakthrough for me was Scream Therapy.

CATHY
Scream Therapy.

NIGEL
Yeah, Scream Therapy-
You know, I just find exerting your voice (is quite a...)

CATHY
We all know how you like exerting your voice, Nigel.

NIGEL
It's a very cleansing experience.

CATHY
(leaning in, confidential)
Look people are listening....
Can we talk about this some other time.

NIGEL
You should try it yourself.

CATHY
Nigel, I don't *need cleansing*.

NIGEL
Go on- try it.

CATHY
No!

This time, Cathy makes a determined move away from Nigel. He just hangs there for a moment. Staring after her.

Cathy moves past Danny as he tackles another couple of innocent bystanders:

>   **DANNY**
> Hey, no, no, listen, pal, before you say anything, you wouldn't have a fiver on you, mate?
>   (waits)
>
>   **DANNY**
> Two quid? I'll pay ya back tomorra, first thing, just tell us where you drink and I'll be there before the doors open...I am owed a hundred, y'know, had a lot of luck at Caulfield last Wednesday...you wanta take a watch as collateral? Transistor radio? No, look, I'll give you the radio and pick it up later on...

But nothing's looking too hopeful with this stingy mob. So Danny collapses back into his seat again, looks around at them.

                      DANNY
    Gawd. What is this, a depression or something?
    No wonder small business is on the skids...eh?
    Where's the justice in that?

He takes another swig of 'Cough Syrup' from his chemist bag, savours it, gargles it, swallows, sighs...and seems to nod off to sleep.

Nigel approaches up to Cathy again. Unable to let her just walk away. Out of his life. Again.
                      NIGEL
    Just grab a lungful and let go.

                      CATHY
    No! Nigel.

NIGEL
The only way out is up, Cathy.

CATHY
I have no intention of making a complete ass of myself in public, thank you very much.

NIGEL
Don't thank me until you've tried it.

CATHY
No!

NIGEL
Air is free, go for it.

CATHY
(warning)
Nigel-

NIGEL
I'll show you.

CATHY
(final warning)
Nigel, don't do it.

Nigel throws back his head and lets out a sudden manic yell.

NIGEL
Ahhhhhhhhhhhhhhhh....

Nigel's yell is echoed by Danny who is shocked out of his nap down the back.

                    DANNY
    Ahhhhhhhhhhhh

                    CATHY
    Christ!

Danny has shot bolt upright and grips a hand strap to stop himself falling forwards into a group of passengers opposite. Alice spots him as she jerks herself up from dusting under some people's seats down the front.

                    ALICE
            (swinging around, confused, concerned)
    Who did that?
    Who made that noise!

She looks from one passenger to another. Finally spots Danny, literally hanging there, holding the strap. She rounds on him.

ALICE
You think it's smart, yelling out like that?

DANNY
(all innocent)
Like what?

ALICE
(almost cracking up, tearful)
Look, this is my first night, you know, and you're not giving me much of a chance are you? You'll have Tran back out here in a minute and...he mightn't be an airline pilot but he's got the same responsibility...you realize that?
(poking her feather duster into his chest)
Your life is his responsibility.
And mine.
And theirs.
(indicating the rest of the tram)
And if he gives me a bad report tonight I'm finished.

DANNY
(looking around at them)
'Strewth.

ALICE
I just wish you'd realize it.

Alice moves away to resume her dusting.
Meanwhile, up the other end, Cathy has totally
distanced herself from Nigel.

DANNY
Driver? ... the man obviously suffers from
Parallelotosis.
(to Alice)
You know what that is, love?
Too much staring at parallel lines. That's *his* problem.

Alice comes back and threatens Danny with the
feather duster again.
Shaking it in his face.

DANNY
(singing - badly -
to the tune of *"Come On Aussie"*)
Bong on Aussie, bong on, bong on...Bong on Aussie...

ALICE
I'm not a bloody Aussie, alright!

SAM
(backing her up)
Here, here.

Alice storms off and Danny resumes drinking his 'cough medicine'.
He chats away to nobody in particular.

DANNY
Ah well - time for a bit of afternoon tea...
(laughs, gargles the mixture,
swallows, coughs uncontrollably)

But his cough is full of bit of a phlegm again - so he's forced to look round for a place to spit and decides to swallow instead.

DANNY
Sometimes I really resent my job-
Being an intellectual, an enlightened one.
Bloody hard sometimes. Being always right.
Up against the excrement life hurls at you.

(sighs)
Yep. I've had a *Fraser* of a day.
(chuckles)

He glances around him, checking out a passenger or two.
Looking for a reaction. Wondering who the Liberals in his audience might be.

DANNY
Eh?
(laughs)
Fraser eh? Malcolm... friggen... Fraser.

DANNY
What a joke!
Life...life...wasn't meant to be...
(long pause, sighs)
...easy.
He was right about that sure enough.
Life *is* like a shit sandwich.
The more bread you have the less crap you eat.
(winks at someone)
Eh? Reckon old Mal's got a bit of parallelotosis as well.
Life begins to lose its meaning. Their hands get all clammy and they sweat a lot...that far away look...and then the sudden burst of anger.
In my considered opinion it's a global medical problem...parallelotoxis.

He never quite says it the same way and drifts off again, quietly whistling the tune to 'Come on Aussie, come on come on..." Taunting Alice who chooses not to listen.

During Danny's rave Nigel has been tentatively making one final pitch to Cathy.

NIGEL
You've got to talk through your emotions more, Cathy.

CATHY
Look, Nigel, it's pretty obvious to me that you've landed in a place where in order to be interesting you've got to appear neurotic.

NIGEL
Well ! What have you been doing? Stuck out here in Sullivans-ville ?
I mean live in Melbourne, 840 billion blow flies can't be wrong.

Cathy comes straight out with it.

CATHY
Nigel, you don't *do* much with two kids in primary school.

This is a bit of a shock.

NIGEL
Two kids?
(frowns)
I didn't know that.

CATHY
No, well you didn't write did you?

NIGEL
(still can't believe it)
Two kids.

CATHY
Boys.

NIGEL
What are you tying yourself down for?

CATHY
Why do you reckon?

Nigel thinks about it for a moment.

NIGEL
You mean they were...unplanned?
(it sounds distasteful

Again, Cathy becomes acutely aware of the people around them.

CATHY
I'd really like to talk about it some other time, Nigel.

There's a slight pause.

NIGEL
How old?

CATHY
Darryl's six and a half and Michael's five.

Nigel does some quick sums.

NIGEL
Six and a half?

CATHY
Yes. Six and a half.

NIGEL
You mean, six months after I left?

CATHY
Darryl was born on the 11th of November 1975.

DANNY
(piping up from down the back)
That's a day to remember, love.

NIGEL
You're kidding!

He stares at her, hoping for a moment that this is all a bad dream.

NIGEL
You're pulling my leg.

CATHY
I don't think pulling your leg had much to do with it.

NIGEL
Come on, Cathy...who
(feeble laugh)
I mean...Who ah, who's the lucky guy?

                    CATHY
          Who do you reckon?

The penny finally drops. Nigel just hangs there, nodding, slack jawed.

                    NIGEL
                    (frowns)
          You never told me this.

Again, she's aware of people listening.

                    CATHY
                    (loud whisper)
          Nigel, I really don't want to talk about this in public if you don't mind!

                    NIGEL
          Six years later I get on a tram and you tell me I'm A FATHER!
                    (looks away)
          I'm going to need another primal...

                    CATHY
                    (warning)
          NO! Nigel -

                    NIGEL

This time Nigel moves away and Cathy follows for a change.

                    NIGEL
          It's therapy, Cathy, I need to scream.

                    CATHY
          Nigel, please don't yell out again.

NIGEL
I'm experiencing a flush of anxiety here you know?
It's very traumatic for me. If I don't let go it can scar

CATHY
(groans)
I you *do* let go I'll make sure you're scarred.

NIGEL
I have to express it.

CATHY
(here we go again)
Oh god!

NIGEL
You've got to admit this is all a bit of a shock.

CATHY
(screams)
Forgodsake, Nigel, just settle down and get a grip on yourself.

Nigel is pacing up and down again but he is obviously used to this tone from Cathy, he recovers a bit, clenching and unclenching his fists, breathing deeply.

CATHY
Yes, yes, do your breathing…it's alright. Nothing can hurt you.

Again Danny pipes up from down the back. Sending Nigel up.

DANNY
That's better.

NIGEL
(starts pacing)
Two kids?
Well they're not both mine.
You can't pin the second one on me.

CATHY
Nigel, we're talking about children, not medals.

NIGEL
Well they're not both mine are they!

CATHY
The youngest one's Jonno's.
(still a little embarrassed about it)
We had a...sort of relationship...for a while...after you left.

NIGEL
You're kidding!
You - and Jonno !

DANNY
Who's Jonno ?

NIGEL
He's a real estate agent!

Cathy is impatient, Nigel is beginning to really bug her again.

CATHY
Yes. I had a relationship with Jonno. Alright.

NIGEL
Oh sure, sure...

                    CATHY
At least he knew what day of the week the garbage got put out.

                    DANNY
Well that's important.

They just ignore Danny.

                    NIGEL
                (still incredulous)
Cathy, you're making this up as you go along.
                (offers his arm)
Pinch me. Go on, pinch me. I've got to be dreaming. This is worse than my last scene breakdown.

                    CATHY
Look, I actually happen to like Jonno, do you mind?

                    NIGEL
                (cynical)
Oh yeah,

                    CATHY
He helps me out.

                    NIGEL
                (not buying it)
Oh sure-

                    CATHY
You try living on the supporting parent's benefit, see how far you go.

                    NIGEL
You don't live with him?

                    CATHY
We can't, can we, I'd lose 98.50 a week.

Nigel is being slightly haughty. The more he thinks about it the more absurd it seems.

NIGEL
You really mean to tell me - there's two kids hanging out in Deepdene, one looks like Jonno, the other looks like me?

CATHY
Darryl's a rather sickly child.

NIGEL
Cathy-

CATHY
And I'm sorry, but I really don't want to talk about this…(in public!)

DANNY
(obviously enjoying himself)
Talk about it, talk about it.

NIGEL
Oh well, yes, we'll just *postpone* it shall we?
(obviously a sore point)
Put it all off till another time…
You're pivoting out on me again, Cathy.

CATHY
Here we go…

NIGEL
Like the flat we were going to get?

Cathy pointedly ignores him, turns away, refusing any more engagement with him.

NIGEL
You won't face the emotional truth of it, will you?

CATHY
I've faced the emotional truth of it for the last six years, do you mind!

NIGEL
Cathy -

Nigel goes to grab her arm, but she swings away putting distance between them. (Not easy in a crowded tram)

CATHY
I don't want to talk about it, Nigel. And that's final.

NIGEL
(being reasonable)
Cathy, how can we solve this if we don't want to talk about it?

DANNY
Talk about it. Talk about it.

But they ignore him as Cathy really hammers into Nigel.

CATHY
Look, stop projecting your hostility onto me.

NIGEL
Right, right, now you're getting the hang of it. "Hostility" is good.

Down the back of the tram Samantha has approached Alice again as the conductress continues to polish away at the metal bits of her tram, while occasionally giving people's shoe's a bit of a shine with her feather duster as she passes by.

SAM
I'm sorry, but I simply can't understand why you put up with it.

ALICE
Well...My teacher at the depot did warn us it could get a bit lively at times.

SAM
Lively!? I think it's criminal that a young girl should be exposed to such harassment. Does your mother know the kind of danger you're in?

ALICE
I haven't actually seen Mum for four years.

SAM
(shocked)
Four years!

ALICE
Yeah, she's been ...
(a little coy about admitting it)

... in Fairleigh.

SAM
(brightens)
Oh that's nice. Where's that?

ALICE
Prison.

SAM
(reacts - shocked)
Oh...oh...how awful.

ALICE
Well she had to find some way to support eight kids.
What with Dad and his crook back and that.

SAM
Eight ! Children!
What an *appalling* upbringing you must have had.

ALICE

Oh no- I was the lucky one. You see I'm the one who got the job. Dad always wanted us to follow the straight and narrow and I thought: "tram tracks". How straight and narrow can you get?

SAM

Well, yes, I do quite admire your determination to pull yourself up by the bootstraps so to speak, but you're so vulnerable here, I mean look around you, you've absolutely no choice about who you let in.
(scanning the other passengers, curling her lip)

ALICE

Oh, this is a relatively quiet trip really...

While Sam and Alice have been talking Cathy is coming back at Nigel, just so it's clear:

CATHY

I am NOT neurotic, okay?

NIGEL
(cynically)

Not neurotic, huh? Then how come you're dressed up like that.

CATHY

Like what?

NIGEL

Like some New Zealand barmaid.

CATHY

I'm going to work.

NIGEL
(still dubious)

Work? Where?

CATHY
Bubbles

NIGEL
Bubbles! What's that?

CATHY
It's a bath house and detox centre. I do deep tissue massage.

NIGEL
(double take/shock)
You what!?

DANNY
Keeps a bit of fruit on the sideboard, eh love?

Nudges someone next to him, winks, taps is nose.

CATHY
How else do you reckon I could afford the fees?

NIGEL
Fees? For What?

CATHY
I'm sending Darryl to Pious College.

NIGEL
(disgusted)
Pious College! My ex-lover is rubbing oil into sweaty, overweight stockbrokers so my son can go to some sick bastion of the authoritarian class?

DANNY
You poor bugger.

CATHY
I'm trying to save him from a life like yours.

NIGEL
And in the process completely alienate him from his natural father.

CATHY
I think we should spare him the shock don't you?

NIGEL
Aren't you at least going to let me see the kid?

CATHY
Ah God, Nigel, you're really amazing aren't you.

NIGEL
Where is he now?

CATHY
At home with mum.

NIGEL
(rising panic)
Your MOTHER!!!
She's living here too?

CATHY
She moved down from Brisbane six months ago ... to help me out.

Nigel has been feeling a sudden rising in the pit of his stomach, he rushes to a doorway and lets out a blood curdling yell.

NIGEL
YOUR MOTH-AAAAAAAAHHHHHHHHHH!!!

Down the other end Danny is caught off guard, and echo's Nigel's scream out of fright...Again...

DANNY
AAAAAAAAHHHHHHHHHH!!!

...before falling back into the hand straps, almost landing on top of somebody.

Alice, distracted from her cleaning again and caught off guard by the noise, suddenly swings round looking for the source. Just as Cathy passes putting as much distance between herself and Nigel as possible.

ALICE
(angry)
Who was that?
(rounding on Danny)
Was that you again?

DANNY
Who? Me?

ALICE
I warned you about disturbing people.

DANNY
I haven't done anything.

Alice spots the bottle of 'cough medicine' hanging out of one pocket.

ALICE
What's this you've got?

DANNY
(trying to hide it)
Nothin'.

ALICE
There's no alcohol allowed. No alcohol allowed!!

DANNY
That's alright. I heard you the first time.
(jerking his head)
' Heard you the first time.

Alice pulls at the bottle, Danny pulls back.

ALICE
I'm confiscating this under section 27 subsection (b) of the Tramways Regulations Act of 1913.

DANNY
(protesting)
But it's only cough medicine.

The tug of war continues.

ALICE
(angry, desperate)
Give it to me!

DANNY
Just my luck to cop a Presbyterian connie.

ALICE
(almost crying)
Please let go.

84

Danny finally lets go.

                DANNY
Alright, alright, I can't stand to see a woman cry.

                ALICE
One more disturbance and you're off. OFF!

                DANNY
Go on, shove it in ya pouch kanga, and thanks for nothin'.
I'll send you a bill for the flu I'm about to get.

                ALICE
Look! I'm on probation, right. Do you realize that? This is my first night solo and if anything goes wrong I could lose my job!

Alice moves brusquely away, coming past Samantha. She has clearly lost some of her earlier enthusiasm for the job. And Feels compelled to explain

ALICE
(to Samantha)
Anyway, I'm not going to be a connie forever.

SAM
I can quite see why.

ALICE
When I've saved enough money I'm going overseas.

SAM
Oh. How wonderful. Where to?

ALICE
Tasmania.

SAM
(how déclassé)
Oh-

ALICE
Of course, I'd love to afford Hollywood, but that could take years.

SAM
Oh, but my dear, some of my best friends have been to Hollywood and they're really *so* two-dimensional. Always boasting about the place.
Like it was the centre of the world. I simply can't abide people who go on and on and on about their travels in public.
(getting louder)
In those terribly ignorant, loud voices that they have.

Alice is glancing around at her passengers. Realising they're all listening to this too. Sam has a very loud and pronounced Eastern Suburbs, Melbourne upper class accent.

SAM
And besides, you never know who's listening.

Alice sneaks a quiet glance sideways at the people listening. Self conscious and a bit embarrassed for Sam.

SAM
No. No, some people are just too shallow and materialistic.

DANNY
That's very socialist of you, love to say so.

SAM
I'm a *socialite*, not a socialist.

Danny laughs and sneaks out a second bottle of 'cough medicine' and quietly taking a few sips, conscious of hiding it from Alice.

DANNY
(indicating Alice up the other end with Sam,
twirling a finger around his temple)
Reckon she's got a bit of parallelo about her that girl.
(to no one in particular)
You can hypnotize a chicken with a straight line, did you know that?
(just raving)
Well here's to public transport, eh?
(another swig)
I think its *absolutely* marvelous. The people you meet…the view…
You see a totally different city from a tram window, don't you think?
The kiddies crying and all of us here,
Why, we're just like tourists in our own home town.

> **DANNY (cont.)**
> See, you don't need to go overseas to find excitement.
> It's all here in our own backyard...so to speak...
> Or my backyard, being a gentleman between
> residences at the moment...

Behind Danny, in one of the doorways, Nigel is quietly trying to light a joint.

> **DANNY**
> ...trapped between parallel lines...

The tram stops again and Terry Meagher rushes on, pulling a large plastic dog behind him, one used for collecting money for the Blind Society. A broken lock and chain dangles from around its neck and a pair of old sunglasses have been taped to the side of the dog's head.

> **TERRY**
> Come on, Bozo, let's go - let's get outta here.
> (urgently tugging the cord)

Terry is dressed like a punk, he's hyper and menacing. He glares at a passenger.

> **TERRY**
> Wanna buy a dog?
> The perfect animal for the family that doesn't like pets.

When they don't look too interested.

> **TERRY**
> No? He's very house trained, and doesn't eat much.

88

The passenger wisely avoids any interaction. So Terry moves on.

                        TERRY
        Okay, Bozo, lets go walkies...

Terry drags the dog along behind him as he moves up the tram.

                        TERRY
                (turning to a passenger)
    Wanna buy a dog?

Then he deliberately bumps Bozo into Samantha's back.
She screams and jumps away. He thinks it's a huge joke.

                        SAM
                (rounding on him)
    Where ever did you get that !?

                        TERRY
Get what?

                        SAM
That dog, you've stolen it!

Terry swings round to notice Bozo, as if for the first time. He jumps away in mock shock.

                        TERRY
Ah!
            (back to Samantha)
Where did he come from?

                        SAM
You've taken that dog from its rightful owners.

Behind Terry (while he remains fully focused on Sam), Danny starts playing with the dog. He takes out an old wire coat-hanger, makes it into a loop, and pretends to get the dog to jump through it.

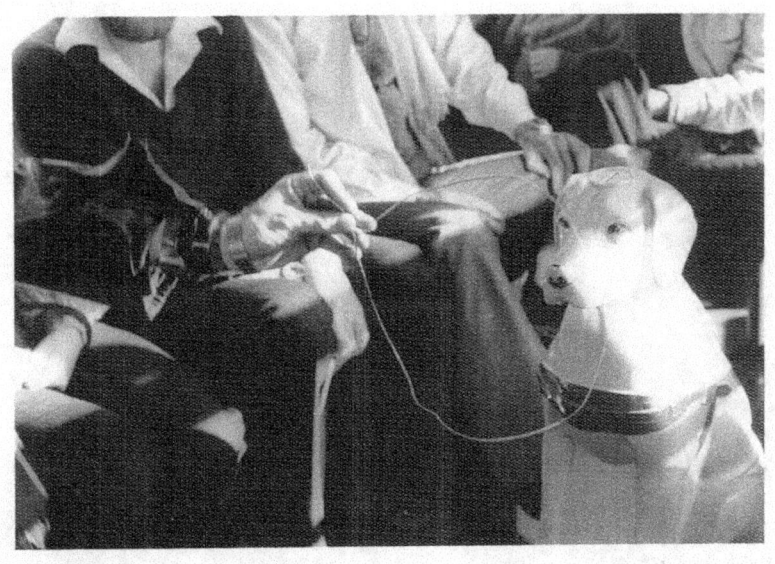

Unaware of this, Terry focuses his full attention on Samantha. An intimidating stare.

TERRY
What makes you say that, lady ?

She hesitates as she takes in the black lipstick and various inventive body piercings. But feels compelled to stand up for her old charity.

SAM
I've worked for the Blind Society and I know they certainly wouldn't give a dog like that to somebody like you.

TERRY
(sneering)
Waddayew mean: "somebody like me"?

SAM
(faltering)
Somebody like you...

TERRY
Yeah? So?

SAM
So...

TERRY
So he followed me here, didn't he?

SAM
But that's ridiculous he can't even walk!

TERRY
No! He can't see. That's why I'm taking him home.

As Sam continues to back away from Terry he keeps a close distance, almost pushing her in front of him through his intimidating posture.
While Danny takes the opportunity to quietly lift the dog upside down.
Then he shakes it, trying to get coins to fall out of the slit in the top of its head.

SAM
What are you rebelling against?

TERRY
Waddayew got?

SAM
I mean why all the black?
Are you in mourning or something?
Has someone just died in your family?

TERRY
Yeah, me poor old mum.

SAM
(melts a little, suddenly sympathetic)
Oh - how, how... unfortunate.

TERRY
(manic look with wide rolling eyes)
Yeah, I just topped her with a chainsaw out in Broady. She really got on my goat.

Even Sam knows that must be bullshit. But she goes on backing away. Not sure how seriously to take Terry.

SAM
So, is that part of the cult to wear your hair like that? It must've cost a fortune...My perms are over a hundred and fifty these days...No, no, I am interested - from a sociological point of view...you see...I did an essay once, at La Trobe...on social deviates...

TERRY
Oh, you're studying me are ya, love?

SAM

No, no, really...ah...just from an anthropological....

TERRY

Well this is what we do...
 (he goes to grab her and kiss her on the cheek)

Sam reels back from his mock embrace.

SAM

Stop it, stop it! How dare you!
I can't bear to be handled by somebody I haven't been introduced to!

TERRY
 (holding out his hand)
The name's Mickey Mouse, love, what's yours.

SAM
 (resisting shaking hands)
Samantha Hart-Byrne and I know that dogs are not allowed on trams.

TERRY
(mock hurt)
Don't listen, Bozo.

Terry swings around to reassure the dog, and spots Danny's holding him upside down. Still shaking.

TERRY
HEY! Derro!

Danny freezes. Terry marches straight up to him. Threatening.

TERRY
Whaddayew think you're doing?

DANNY
I was only trying to teach him a back flip.

Terry grabs Danny in an arm lock, twisting his elbows up while rummaging through his pockets for anything valuable.

DANNY
Hey, I had a few quid in there.

TERRY
I'd like you help you out, pal, but you smell a bit woofy.

DANNY
(growling at him)
Get out of it, ya young punk.

TERRY
Had a few drinks, have ya mate?

DANNY
(struggling)
Let go!

TERRY
Had a few drinks with ya mates after work?

DANNY
I don't work, I think.

TERRY
'Course you do, it's dribbled all over you. See...

Terry does the old trick of pointing to the middle of Danny's chest. As Danny looks down, Terry flips his finger up into Danny's face. Slapping his nose.
Terry thinks it's a huge joke, bends over laughing, cracking up. Danny is furious.

DANNY
(pushing him away)
Get out of it! Ya punk bastard...

Egged on quietly by Sam, Alice has finally summoned up enough courage to confront Terry head on.

ALICE
Fares, thanks.

Terry stops dead in his tracks, does a really slow turn and his eyes light up like poker machines when you hit the jackpot...as he slowly takes in Alice from head to foot.

TERRY
Oh, you... are.... *be - u - ti - ful*!

Alice looks extremely dubious. Inwardly scoffing at his silly act. But holding her ground.
TERRY
(exaggerated emotion)
I *lo-ve* you !

Danny backs away from Terry, glad that his attention is now focused on someone else. He starts fiddling with his transistor radio again, switching it on and shaking it, trying to get it to work. Figuring it must be time for the race at Moonee Valley.

ALICE
(standing her ground, but ready to call the driver)
Fares thanks.

TERRY
How much *are* you love?

ALICE
Depends where you want to go.

TERRY
All the way if you're comin...

ALICE
It's a dollar ten to the city.

TERRY
Gee - you're cheap.

She slaps him. Hard.

ALICE
How dare you!

Terry's eyes roll around, exaggerating the power of her slap. His knees go wobbly.

TERRY
Oh, I *love* it when you do that.

Terry notices Danny still fiddling with the radio.

TERRY
Hey, derro. Get something romantic on that thing, I think I'm falling in love...

Samantha groans audibly. Terry wrenches the radio off Danny, switches it on, music fills the air.

DANNY
It works!

Terry keeps moving towards her.

ALICE
(finally annoyed)
Oh rack off.

TERRY
Doncha want to dance then?

SAM
(groans, rolls her eyes)
Oh really!

ALICE
I'm warning you, Tran Van Minh has a black belt in tae-kwon-do.
(pointing to the driver's door)
He'll be out here in a minute.

TERRY
Got a scene with him or something?
(coming towards her, holding the radio up,
swaying to the music)

Danny takes the opportunity of Terry's focus on Alice to scoop up the plastic dog and pull the cord for the next stop, intending to sneak off with it.

ALICE
And please turn that down...you're not allowed to interfere with other passengers.

TERRY
Well, have ya darlin'?

Samantha feels compelled to speak up.

SAM
Why don't you just leave her alone.

TERRY
I'm only trying to be friendly.

ALICE
And I'm trying to do my job. Alright!

SAM
Here, here.

The tram stops and Terry notices Danny about to escape with the dog. He charges right up to Danny and swings him round.

TERRY
Hey, where do you think you're going?

Terry grabs the dog back.

DANNY
(sprung)
What?

TERRY
Want to get off, derro?

DANNY
Well, you took my radio.

TERRY
(pushing him)
Off you go then...

Terry stamps on his foot. Danny erupts with a yelp of pain.

DANNY
(screaming/hopping around)
Oh God! The other foot !!

ALICE
(to Danny)
Right I warned you about yelling out like that. Under section 95 of paragraph B of subsection 7 of the 1913 Act, I'm ordering you to please leave my tram immediately.

TERRY
He wants to go anyway.

DANNY
(moving away from the door)
I've paid me fare, I'm not budging.

ALICE
You haven't paid your fare you haven't paid anything. You owe me a dollar ten.

DANNY
A dollar ten! Crikey!

ALICE
Either you pay or - off! - off!

DANNY
There you go, re- re- repeating yourself again, again, again...

ALICE
(insistent)
A dollar ten

DANNY
Gawd, its more oppressive than Queensland.

Danny is rummaging through his various pockets, locating the odd coin. He starts counting them into her open palm, there's a lot of copper...

DANNY
Thirteen...fourteen...sixteen...twenty three...

ALICE
(picking one coin out)
That's no good.

DANNY
What?

ALICE
(holding it up)
Wrong country

DANNY
Come on that's a furry wombat.

ALICE
It's a New Zealand animal.

TERRY
Okay, so it migrated here. Didn't it?

ALICE
Yeah well, I can't take it! We can't take New Zealand coins.

Inexplicably, Terry has come round to Danny's side.

TERRY
Geeze, if you don't like your job, mate, why doncha just chuck it in?

ALICE
I like my job, it's him that's the problem. And you!

Danny gives up counting and drops the rest of a bunch of small coins into her hand, wrapping her fist around them.

DANNY
There you go, love, there you are then.
That ought to cover it.

ALICE
(slowly, deliberately)
That's not enough.

DANNY
It's pretty close.

ALICE
It's nowhere near enough.

DANNY
It's a fair bit.

ALICE
(screams)
I can't take it!

In one swift move she hurls the fistful of copper coins out the doorway.

DANNY
What'd you do that for?

ALICE
Do you know how much a bag full of two cents weighs?

TERRY
(to Alice, pointing out the door)
You owe him a dollar ten, mate.

Danny is hopping around on one leg, tugging at his other shoe.

DANNY
I'll give you a pound, alright?

SAM
Oh please don't take that off.

DANNY
You got change for that, 'cause that's what I'm down to.

He pulls out a pound note neatly wrapped in cellophane, which he's kept in his shoe for a rainy day, probably for some decades.

ALICE
WE CAN'T TAKE POUNDS!

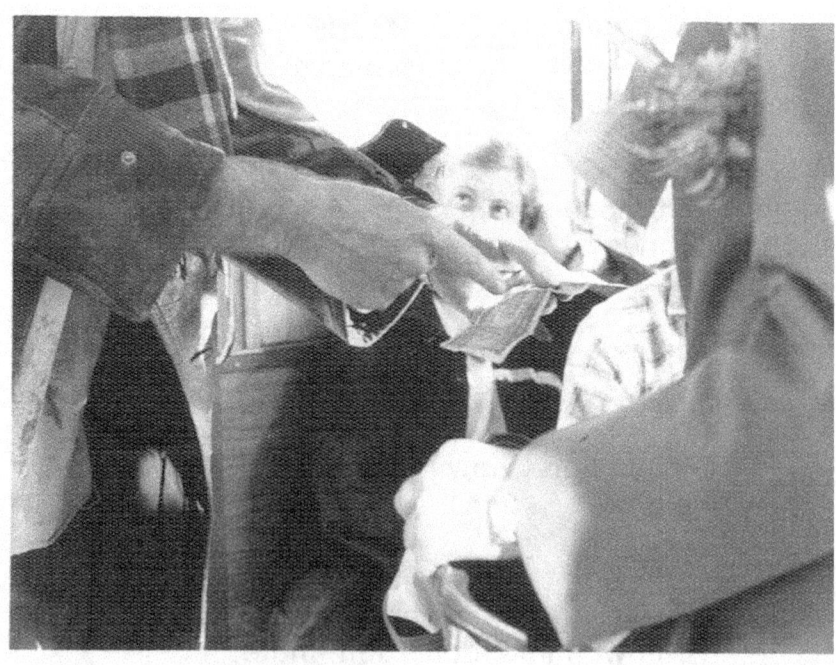

DANNY
I've had this since the royal visit in 1954.
That should cover your lousey dollar ten I reckon.

TERRY
Worth more, probably.

DANNY
Same queen, only younger.

ALICE
We can't take pounds. We gotta have dollars!!

DANNY
Won't take a quid, you're sick, you realize that?

SAM
She's only doing he job, for goodness sake.

DANNY
(rounding on her)
And you lady, oughta be destroyed.

ALICE
Either you buy a ticket or I'm calling an inspector.

DANNY
(turning to a passenger)
Wouldn't be good for a dollar would you mate?

Terry steps up to the plate.

TERRY
Hey, now, come on love, I'll buy the old codger's ticket alright?

DANNY
Ah - thank you very much, that's very kind of you.
(to the others)
Gee, he's almost human, isn't he?

                    TERRY
A dollar ten, is that what you want?

He gives a dollar twenty to Alice.

                    TERRY
    Keep the change.

Danny is delighted at this outcome.

                    DANNY
            (pointing to Terry's hair)
    Hey, you didn't put your finger in a light bulb, did you
    mate, and turn it on?
                    (laughs)

                    TERRY
    Very funny.

Alice clicks a ticket and gives it to Danny. And things tend to quieten down for a moment. Except for Danny's radio.

                    ALICE
    Now would you mind turning the radio off, please.

                    TERRY
    What's wrong with a little music.? I thought we lived in
    a democracy.

                    DANNY
    That's right, what's left of it.

                    ALICE
    Off.

                    TERRY
            (turning to the other passengers)
    What sorta country doesn't like a little muzac on its
    trams?

> ALICE

You're not allowed to disturb other people.

> TERRY

Hey, no swinging the votes.

> ALICE

Right off!

Terry turns it up, then down a little, then up again, teasing her. Enjoying himself. Then up, then down again.

> TERRY

That's not disturbing anyone is it?

Alice just stares hard at him, arms akimbo.

> ALICE

I'm warning you.

Terry teases her with the volume, turning it down slowly, then up again quickly, then down slowly, until, eventually, almost imperceptibly, he switches it off.

Danny reaches over and grabs it.

> DANNY

It's mine anyway.

Terry pulls back.

> TERRY

Hey, I'll give it to you in a minute, mate.

> DANNY
> (urgent, pleading)

The 5th at Mooney Valley is about to start.

TERRY
No radios allowed mate, didn't you hear the lady?

DANNY
It's my tranny, you stole it.

TERRY
Well, you stole my dog you stupid old clown.

Danny makes another grab for the radio.
Terry pulls back. Holding it up out of Danny's reach.

TERRY
Hang, on, hang on... you don't want to break it.

DANNY
(as they struggle)
Ya punk thief, let go!

TERRY
Okay.

Much to Danny's surprise Terry does so, causing
Danny to lose balance and
stagger back.

TERRY
(blowing kisses at him)
But it's only 'cause I love you.

Danny eyes him coolly for a moment.
Terry holds out his hand to help him up.

TERRY
Shake, okay?

Danny isn't sure. But, tentatively, still on the ground, Danny puts out his hand. Terry pulls Danny back to his feet and takes his hand into a vice-like grip.

>DANNY
>Ya squashin' all me knuckles!

>TERRY
>Well, I've got a firm personality.

>DANNY
>LET GO!
>>(pulling back hard)
>Ya punk thug.

>TERRY
>Okay...

Terry lets go and again, Danny reels back, this time crashing into the defensive arms of another passenger, who pushes back.

>TERRY
>>(hugely amused)
>There's no need to hug him.

Danny sprawls onto the floor, lying back, looking up at the unfortunate passenger.

>DANNY
>Sorry, mate.

Terry is laughing outright. Thinks it's a great joke.

>DANNY
>Stuff you ya mongrel.

112
In an instant the laughter stops. And so does the tram.

TERRY
What!?

DANNY
(thoroughly fed up now)
I said stuff off!

Danny staggers back to his feet again, dusting himself off, shaking his tranny against his ear. Trying to get it to go. Desperate to hear his race.

TERRY
I don't think you deserve a free ride.

In one swift movement Terry grabs Danny by the seat of the pants and frog marches him up through the tram to the far doorway. Danny resists, trying to latch onto various poles and perhaps, people. Dropping his tranny into someone's lap...

DANNY

Hey! Hey!
 (reaching out for an anchor, to stop Terry's push)

TERRY

There'll be no bad language on this tram thank you very much.

DANNY

I want to go to Mont Albert!

TERRY

Well off you go then. Start walking...

The door opens and in one swift move Terry grabs Danny by the back of the shoulders and propels him out into the street.

DANNY

Hey, Ya young!... bah!

But before Danny can get his bearings, Terry laughing, pulls the cord to start the tram again. He thinks it's hilarious, and is bent over holding his sides. Cracking up

Out on the street, Danny's protests start to fade as the tram moves off.
The doors close and everyone looks unsettled and a little stunned.

Falling behind, Danny manages to bang on the side of the tram, madly but hopelessly jogging after it.

DANNY
Hey, hey...

DANNY
You BLOODY ANIMAAAAALLLL, BLOOD YOUNG PUNK FASCIST BASTAAAAARRRRDDDDD!!!!

TERRY
Come on Granpa! hurry up!
(Terry mimes a jogging action)
Lift those knees - bit of exercise, do you good.
(back inside the tram, filling them in)
Gone all red in the face he has.
(back out at Danny)
Don't have a heart attack, mate!

Terry thinks it's the funniest thing he's ever seen. The yelling from Danny tapers off as he disappears behind the tram and is left, bent over, grasping his heart, stabbing pain from angina coursing through his body. The last thing passengers see is Danny sinking to his knees on the nature strip in Victoria Parade.

TERRY
Only joggers die young.
You'll probably make the next Olympics.

Finally, the yelling and cursing from Danny recedes into silence.

TERRY
(proudly, smiling back at Alice)
There you are, love. Nice quiet tram for you.

She looks less than impressed as Nigel passes her on route back up to Cathy, who has been maintaining her distance from him at the far end of the tram. He's simply been unable to stand it any longer and takes his heart in his hands.

NIGEL
(sincerely)
I'm...sorry...

CATHY
Look, Nigel...

NIGEL
It was just such a shock...to find out...

CATHY
I'm not perfect, okay? I have to manage, somehow.

NIGEL
It's just that I feel so guilty. The thought of you doing it for money.

CATHY
If you're going to go on about it, I'm getting off right now.

NIGEL
(taking her arm/half a plea)
Come with me - ?

CATHY
(simply)
No.

NIGEL
Come on, we could have a bite to eat somewhere.

CATHY
I'm going to work!

NIGEL
(still appalled)
Work! Is that what you call it!

CATHY
Yes, WORK!

So Nigel backs off. This is not the right approach.

NIGEL
Okay, I'm loose about it.

CATHY

Good.

NIGEL

You're loose about it. I'm loose about it.

CATHY

Good.

NIGEL

You *are*...loose about it?

CATHY

Yes, I'm loose.

In the background Terry listens in, amused by their conversation, quietly sending it up.

NIGEL

Look -

CATHY

What?

NIGEL

Let's have a drink together. Just a quick one...

Lewd gestures from Terry at the phrase "quick one"

TERRY

Ouuuu....

CATHY

No.

NIGEL

Fifteen minutes...
(pleading)

CATHY
I'm busy.

NIGEL
I'll pay you for your time.

CATHY
That'd be a first.

Nigel reaches for his wallet.

NIGEL
Come on, how much are you?

CATHY
Nigel, you couldn't possibly afford it.

NIGEL
(leafing through a few notes)
How much?

CATHY
A hundred and fifty.

NIGEL
(staggered)
A night!
(and just hangs there, wallet open)

CATHY
An hour.

Nigel's jaw drops, he slowly folds his wallet, putting it away.

NIGEL
(gulps)
Will you take a cheque?

CATHY
No.

Cathy pulls the cord to stop the tram.

NIGEL
You can rent a steadycam for less than that.

CATHY
Well, have a drink with a camera,
you're probably made for each other.

Meanwhile Terry has been keeping a keen eye on Alice. Teasing her by silently planting his dirty Doc Martins against the glass window in the doorway. She immediately polishes the smudge away. He chuckles and does it to another panel of glass, then he licks it off with his tongue, until he finally lifts himself upside down in the hand stirrups and plants two dirty smudges on the ceiling. Which she has no chance of reaching.

The tram stops and Cathy moves to exit.

NIGEL
Couldn't you ring in sick or something?

CATHY
We don't get sick pay.

She gets off. He's thinking fast, hovering around her out on the street.

NIGEL
Come on, I love you, there's a lot to talk about.

CATHY
There's nothing to talk about, Nigel. It's 1982.

NIGEL
Two years from 1984!

But she remains unmoved. As they walk off towards her appointment.

NIGEL
Cathy, Cathy, Cathy... its been six years! (forgodsake!)

CATHY
(correcting)
Seven

NIGEL
It's a long time. Rupert Murdoch owns half the world...

Their conversation fades out as they disappear around a corner.

Waiting at the same stop is Morris Stanly. Alice spots him approaching and immediately goes into panic mode. Disengaging completely from Terry.

TERRY
(confused)
What?

ALICE
(panicking)
Shuddup! Just behave!

Alice tries to hide Terry behind her as Morris bounces aboard. He stabs a quick glance round at the passengers, eyes narrowing with suspicion. As far as Morris is concerned all of them are guilty until proven guilty - which is undoubtedly what they are.

Morris quickly moves to occupy the commanding centre of the tram. He wears a large white overcoat tightly buttoned up. His pork pie hat has a couple of tram tickets pinned to the band. He also wears thick glasses. He lets a few people become aware of his odd presence - a couple even have the temerity to snigger at his strange costume. They'll pay for their insolence in due course.

Morris quickly reaches into his overcoat, blows a whistle and produces a large magnifying glass. The whistle has the intended effect of stunning the tram into silence. Having got their attention, Morris opens his coat fully to reveal an inspector's badge and several war medals.

MORRIS
Kindly have your tickets ready, thank you ladies and gentlemen!

While they're getting their tickets out Morris strolls casually up to Alice, tipping the rim of his hat slightly.

MORRIS
Miss Cronin. Very good evening to you.

ALICE
(brightly)
Hullo, Mr. Stanly, sir.

MORRIS
How's your first big night solo going?

ALICE
Good, very good, thank you sir. Great. It's been...quiet and really delightful...to be working for the MMTB tonight, sir. I'm very happy with the way things have been going?

MORRIS
Anything you need to report?

ALICE
(too quickly)
No.

His eyes narrow slightly. Always suspicious.
He takes out a card, ticks off certain squares.

MORRIS
No incidents of a dubious nature? No bad behaviour?

ALICE
None whatsoever. It's been simply fantastic.

MORRIS
Obnoxious passengers? Fare evasion?

ALICE
Nothing.

MORRIS
Acts of vandalism?

ALICE
Nada.

MORRIS
Smoking?

ALICE
Nup.

MORRIS
Counterfeit, obsolete, or foreign currency produced to pay for fares?

ALICE
Not a single note in any currency other than Australian dollars.

MORRIS
(still skeptical)
Bit unusual for a Thursday (adjust) night ?

ALICE
(as if reciting it)
It's been one of the best behaved and most pleasant public transport journeys I've ever had the privilege to serve on, sir.

MORRIS
Well it *is* your first one... One of many, possibly.
(turning to the rest of the tram)
So how's she been treating you all? Eh?

Egged on by Terry, the other passengers voice their approval.

TERRY
(fading into the background, sending him up)
Really well Mr. Stand-ly.

SAM
Alice has been doing a simply wonderful job.

Morris hesitates, looking around for the source of the person mis-quoting his name, polishing his magnifying glass with an equally large handkerchief.

MORRIS
Well let's put that to the acid test, shall we?
(sudden mean twist to his voice)
Kindly have your tickets ready for inspection, thank you ladies and gentlemen.

As people go to retrieve their tickets, Morris starts moving around the tram, checking each one with intense scrutiny though his thick magnifying glass, turning tickets over, holding them up to the light. Occasionally checking the faces of the passengers themselves with the glass. And reacting to various skin defects before handing their tickets back...

MORRIS
Thank you...
Thank you...
Thank you...

Alice's heart sinks as she sees him making his way towards Terry who is standing with the guide dog, having taken the sunglasses off the dog and put them on himself.

Morris reacts as the magnifying glass wanders over the dog. He reels back and takes in Terry. The strange costume, the sunglasses at night, the vacant, fake smile. Morris hesitates a moment, quizzical, suspicious, then beams at him.
Suddenly all sympathy and concern.

MORRIS
Ah, well done, lad! Good to see you out there - in the community, trying...

Morris reaches into a deep coat pocket, selects a few coins and drops them into the dog through the small slit in its skull.

MORRIS
(patting Bozo)
Look after him boy, you're all he's got now.

SAM
(can't contain herself any longer, moves forward)
Inspector!

MORRIS
(slight impatience)
I'll be with you in a minute, madam.

Morris checks a few more passenger's tickets, then pulls up short. Prepared to do business. He's found one!

Morris checks the guilty party with his glass wandering over their face and jewellery. Then stands back, loosens his tie, his voice almost croaky with emotion: the thrill of the chase...He checks the offending ticket with an even more powerful, diamond cutter's eyepiece.

MORRIS
Would you mind telling me when you first purchased this travelcard sir?
(checks his watch for the exact time- it's a two hour card)

SAM
(still appalled that Terry's getting off scott-free)
Inspector, may I have a word...

MORRIS
(impatient)
I said I'll be with you in a minute, madam.

Then turns back to his victim.

MORRIS
Well, sir? Are you positive that you didn't in fact purchase this card on November 14 last year and doctor it subsequently in order to feloniously reuse it again? Possibly numerous times.

Morris fans himself with the said card as the culprit mutters something pathetic about buying it at the terminus earlier this evening...

MORRIS
Could I draw your attention to the state of the November square, sir? And the 14?
(taking out his book of fines, starts writing in it)

While in the background Alice tries to stop Sam from intervening, fearing for her job, almost physically holding her back, pleading in whispers. But Sam can't help herself now that someone with real authority is on board.

SAM
(to Morris)
I'm sorry, but there is a youth on this tram who stole a blind dog, accosted me personally, and just a moment ago pushed an elderly passenger out (the doorway...)

MORRIS
(rounding on her, cutting her off)
Will you SHUT-UP! MADAM!!
(then triumphantly back at the guilty ticket fraudster)
The number 14 has completely disappeared !

The guilty passenger might mumble some feeble protest. Something about buying it this evening.

MORRIS
You expect me to believe that!? What are you running an illegal printing press out there in Mont Albert or something?
(waits)
Well, sir? Are you aware that defacing an MTB travelcard is a punishable offence?

He tears the offending travel card in half and throws it behind him. Disgusted.
(of course all the tickets are exactly the same and this fact may now cause some heightened concern among the rest of the passengers.)

MORRIS
Name and address?
(writes it down)
You'll get your summons in the mail.

Finally Morris has worked his way back around to
Terry, still standing holding his 'blind dog'
>> **ALICE**
>> (final feeble attempt to distract him away from Terry)
>> Mr. Stanley...

>> **MORRIS**
>> (gently to Terry, friendly, smiling)
>> Could I trouble you for your ticket, young man?

Terry fans out a handful of odd cards, playing cards, postcards, old bits and pieces of paper
>> **TERRY**
>> Certainly, pick a card, any card...

Morris looks momentarily taken aback. Samantha still hovering, steps forward again.

SAM
(whipping the sunglasses off Terry)
He did not buy a ticket and he is *NOT* blind!

Morris takes off his own glasses, and leans forward to stare into Terry's eyes. Terry makes like a blind man-groping his hands blindly forward, cheekily pinching Morris's coat, looking for a nipple to squeeze. Morris steps back, agog at the deception. And the impertinence.

MORRIS
(suddenly serious)
Now don't muck around with me, son. Did you buy a ticket?

TERRY
Course I did - ask her.
(indicating Alice)
Ask anyone...

Somehow Morris gets Terry's sunglasses mixed up with his own. He puts the sunglasses back on by mistake, looking around for Alice. Unable to see her in the dark.

MORRIS
Well, miss Cronin?

Then aware of the mistake, angrily thrusts the sunglasses back at Terry, puts his own back on.

ALICE
Well, yes he did buy a ticket, but...

TERRY
Y'see.

                              MORRIS
> But what?

                              ALICE
> Well- but...

                              SAM
> He did not buy one.

Morris is totally confused turning from one to the other.

                              MORRIS
> Well did he or didn't he?!

                              ALICE
> Yes he did - but it was for someone else.

Morris takes a deep breath and slowly, menacingly rounds on Terry.

                              MORRIS
> Now don't make this difficult for me, *son*!

Terry takes out a dollar.
                              TERRY
> Alright, alright...

Morris snaps his fingers, summoning her.

                              MORRIS
> Miss Cronin! Attend to this matter thank you.

Alice comes sheepishly forward, takes Terry's dollar ten, clips a travelcard and hands it back. Morris is shaking his head at her, makes a dark note in his official looking notebook. The black one. Then notices her footwear for the first time (high heeled, multi-coloured platform soles).

                    MORRIS
They're a rather extraordinary pair of shoes, Miss
Cronin. They don't look quite regulation to me.

                    ALICE
Sorry, Mr. Stanley.

                    MORRIS
I'm afraid "sorry" isn't quite good enough. You can
hand me that P plate now thank you very much.

Alarmed at what this means, Alice goes to water.

                    ALICE
Oh please, sir. Please don't...
(she tries to protect it, holding her heart on her sleeve, literally)

But Morris pulls her 'P plate' from its Velcro base on
her uniform and pockets it. Then checks his watch,
and makes another note in his official book.

                    MORRIS
On account of gross dereliction of duty, I'm officially
standing you down as at 8.59 pm precisely...
                    (adjust)

                    ALICE
Please, Mr. Stanly, I've got an invalid mother to
support.
                    MORRIS
                    (unmoved)
After the city shunt you'll take this tram straight back to
Malvern Depot and hand in your uniform.

                    ALICE
                (breaking down)
NO!
                    TERRY
Great, now you can come out with me.

Alice stabs daggers at Terry with her eyes. But is too caught up in her own predicament.

MORRIS
And may I add what a great disappointment you've been to me personally, Miss Cronin. I had high hopes you know...
(shrugs)
Oh well, life wasn't mean to be easy.

ALICE
(almost spitting it at Terry)
Thanks for nothing.

TERRY
(protesting back)
You cost me a dollar ten.

ALICE
(through tears)
And I just lost my job!!

Alice sinks to her knees and collapses into the arms of a nearby passenger, sobbing uncontrollably.

Ignoring all that Morris turns back to the rest of the passengers.

MORRIS
Ladies and gentlemen...permit me to *expose* myself to you for a moment.

He takes off his hat and glasses, a slight bow.

MORRIS
(proudly)
Morris Stanley. Chief Super-intendant of Timetables at the MMTB and...
(coyly)
Part time creative author - largely responsible for this evening's little diversion.

Morris takes a small bow in acknowledgement of the scattered applause.

MORRIS

Now I've had a bit of trouble with people walking out on my shows in the past and I'd just like you to know that...

He starts mopping the perspiration from inside the rim of his hat with his ever present hankie, in fact there are dark patches from perspiration in the armpits of his overcoat - Morris seems to perspire quite a lot.

MORRIS
...this time, I've cleverly positioned interval to occur a full thirteen and a half kilometers from where you've parked your cars! So if you're thinking of leaving this one you've got a jolly long walk ahead of you!
(then on a calmer note)

MORRIS (cont)
If you choose to remain and witness the exciting climax to our little reverie this tram will be returning to the Elizabeth Street stop in precisely 29 minutes and 31 seconds. Should you require refreshment in the meantime liquid beverages are available from the Australia Hotel in fashionable downtown Collins Street, the Paris of the Southern Hemisphere, where- on presentation of your travelcards you will receive one or two cups of coffee absolutely free. The person whose card I tore in half will receive half a cup of coffee.
(disapprovingly)
Alcohol may be purchased, but I must stress, unless you are back at the Elizabeth Street stop in precisely now
(checks watch)
twenty eight minutes and thirty seven seconds you will miss the entire second half of the show. Latecomers cannot physically be admitted - unless they hire a cab to catch up, which has happened -
(notices someone glancing out a window)

> Excuse me, are you listening?
>> So, to this end we will now synchronise our watches.
>> On the third beep it will be eleven twenty one and...

Morris trails off, people are laughing, that doesn't seem right. He puts his watch to his ear. It's stopped! His blustering confidence evaporates.

MORRIS
(sudden humility)
Oh...oh...has anybody got the time?

People shout out the time, some are out by several minutes. General confusion. This is cut through by Sam's sudden outcry.

SAM
Oh!

She's anxiously looking through a window to the street outside.

SAM
They've all gone in !

MORRIS
(perplexed)
What?

SAM
Stop! Stop the tram!

Alice pulls the cord for her.

MORRIS
What's...going on?

SAM
I'm late you moron, thank you for nothing.

MORRIS
(sudden dawning realization)
Oh you're leaving are you?

SAM
I'm writing to my local member. A personal friend. And next in line to become Transport Minister. I want him to know this is the most upsetting public journey I've ever been on!
(correcting)
Well, yes, alright, it is the first one. But it's had a positively awful effect on my nerves.

MORRIS

> (pained restraint)
> And where is madam going, may one ask?

SAM
To the Melbourne Theatre Company.

MORRIS
(explodes)
MELBOURNE THEATRE COMPANY!!!

SAM
Yes, I'm going to see *Cuckold In The Nest*
(adjust to whatever is on)

MORRIS
CUCKOLD IN THE NEST !!!
What's wrong with my little show?

The tram stops opposite the Melbourne Theatre Company in Collins Street.

SAM
(contemptuous)
It speaks for itself.

The doors open and Sam sweeps off, triumphant into the night. Morris moves quickly to the open door, shouting out after her.

MORRIS
Not good enough for you, eh?
Oh yes, Oh yes.

Passers-by react. But unperturbed Samantha crosses the street and moves up into the Athenaeum theatre.

MORRIS
Go on. Go off to your boring proscenium arch melodrama. See if I care!
> (almost choking on the words)

Melbourne Theatre Company!
> (then back at her again)

Don't you realize what an adventure in performative realism this is!?

MORRIS (cont)
> (inside the tram –
> appealing directly to other passengers)

What's wrong with exciting, innovative, documentary theatre, huh?
Done on location.
> (out at Sam again, a manic yell)

You're by-passed, lady. By-passed!!
I hope you drop your Jaffas.
If you'd brought a broom you could've flown here.

As the tram moves on Sam disappears from view and Morris turns his attention back to his, once again, diminishing audience. He clutches his chest, mopping his brow, suddenly exhausted. Short of breath.

MORRIS
Excuse me if I seem a trifle distant from time to time ladies and gentlemen.
> (weeps it)

Cuckold In The Nest.

MORRIS

It's just that I have a slight flutter of the heart and a tendency to perspire a lot. Has anyone got a valium? Aspros? I'll take Panadene...No?
No, I suppose not.
> (flash of anger again, bitter)

There's always someone who "walks" isn't there? Doesn't she realize the Australia Council have just cut us off. Again! I mean we're so poor we can't even afford our own theatre. We've got to do the bloody show on a tram forgoodnessake! And now I've got to take you off to a borrowed hotel for interval. We haven't even got our own bar! People have no idea of the sacrifices an artist makes. I could have been a great detective.

The tram stops at Elizabeth Street. Morris pulls himself together.

MORRIS
Right, here's Elizabeth street. Everyone off thank you. Please break down in to groups of two or three as you walk back towards the Australia Hotel. Keep up a little animated conversation about the show and try to pretend that you're not all from Mont Albert. This *is* a fashionable part of town. Right. All off, all change here thank you...

As Morris passes Terry on the way out he reaches for the 'blind dog'. Terry resists.

MORRIS
I put forty cents in there.

TERRY
What a cheapskate.

MORRIS
I'm confiscating this dog on behalf of the Blind Society.

As they stand in the doorway struggling over the dog, people exit the tram around them.

TERRY
I paid over a dollar to go two stops.

MORRIS
I've a good mind to report you to the RSPCA.

Morris finally wrenches the dog free from Terry and carries it with him as he hurries to catch up with his audience, directing them towards the hotel.

MORRIS
Please cross at the traffic lights ladies and gentlemen. We lost three pensioners last week to a stolen car. I mean it's all very well to start with a full house but when you come back three down at half time plays havoc with the bookkeeping.

INTERVAL

Interval takes place at the Australia Hotel in Collins Street where the audience is lead by Morris. Meanwhile the tram with Alice still on board shunts at the end of Swanston Street and waits there approximately half an hour

ACT TWO

RETURN (OUTWARD) JOURNEY

Approximately half an hour later (depending on CBD traffic flows) the tram has shunted at its city terminus and arrives back at the Elizabeth Street corner in Collins Street, heading in the opposite direction - away from the city and back towards Mont Albert.

As the audience get back on, Morris assumes a central position in the tram, overseeing their arrival.

MORRIS
Ladies and gentlemen, the seat allocation is as follows: Liberal voters up the front, Labour to the rear and Independents and Greenies on the running board...
(a broad, if ghastly smile)
Only joking.
No- the main thing is: are there any members of the general public on board? Anyone who hasn't got one of these odd travel cards?
(holding up the special travel card/show ticket)

He waits for any response.

MORRIS
I'm warning you, you're in for shock if you haven't...
(finally)
Are there any *normal* people here?
(mild laughter)
Oh good, lets get on with it shall we?
(turning to Alice)
Miss Cronin, take this tram and these good people straight back to the Mont Albert terminus and then to the depot where you will hand in your uniform and collect your severance pay.

Alice almost chokes again at the thought she's lost her job. Serenely, Morris opens his copy of *Crime and Punishment* magazine and Alice sadly pulls the cord to start the tram for the last time - just as Terry jumps back on board, carrying a banjo, smoking a rollie. Her heart sinks. Him again! She ignores him by polishing some glass panels with a her can of "Windex". He taps her shoulder, she swings round.

TERRY

Hey, no- listen...before you say anything I just wanted you to know how I felt, like...before...when you dobbed me in.

He ignores him, turns back to her polishing.

TERRY

I thought you could make it up to me by coming for a game of Space Invaders...? Like, after you finish...There's this place near the depot...

For answer she sprays out his cigarette with her Windex. He reacts with a grunt.

TERRY
Ahh!!

Terry exaggeratedly wipes the Windex out of his eyes, realizes she probably isn't into Space Invaders.

TERRY
Well what about the "Underground" then?

No response.

TERRY
The "Metro" ?

She goes on polishing glass.

TERRY
Just one game... A dance? Anything...

ALICE
I'm sorry, but I feel a bit washed out after a broken shift like this.

MORRIS
(glancing up from his magazine)
Well I'm not surprised - in those high heels, they're not exactly regulation are they?

ALICE
Plus I just lost my job in case you hadn't noticed. I can't afford to go anywhere.

TERRY
Great, then you've got plenty of time. We'll catch a band or something

ALICE
I'm sorry, I'm so depressed I just want to go home to bed.

TERRY
(moving in on her, putting an arm around)
Okay.

ALICE
(pushing him away)
By myself!

TERRY
Well how about tomorrow night?

ALICE
I'll be looking for another career tomorrow.

TERRY
The weekend?

ALICE
I'm on standby for a cleaning job.

TERRY
(getting the message)
You mean stand-off, don't you?

ALICE
Look, I don't want to go out with you, clear!?

Terry looks mock-hurt.

TERRY
That what you want to do all your life? Clean windows, get hassled by ratbags?

ALICE
I'm being hassled now!

Terry swings the banjo off his shoulder and strums a few chords.

ALICE
Where did you steal that?

TERRY
Bozo's a retriever.

ALICE
And where is Bozo ?

TERRY
He just got retrieved.
Hey what are you doing next month, then?

Alice gives up and stashes away her cloth and bottle of Windex into a box of cleaning materials.

ALICE
Look! I may seem like an ordinary connie to you. But I'm not! This job meant more to me than anything else in the world. I'm passionately committed to the whole idea of trams. One day there won't be any other form of transport. No cars.

Terry strikes a cord.

ALICE
No busses.
       (a cord)
No planes.

ALICE (cont)
(a cord)
No trains
(a cord)
Just... club trams, dining trams, cargo trams, two-hundred-a-kilometer-an-hour trams (like they have in Japan).
(a riff of cords)
Trams to Sydney
(a cord)
And trams to Perth
(a cord)

Accompanied by Terry on banjo, Alice swings into a song and dance routine to the tune of "When I go to Rio"

ALICE
(sings)
Whe-e-e-n...the...driver,
When the driver smiles at me
I go to Richmond-
Or to Balwyn-
I got my tie on,
My suit and smile on,
Got both shoes on,
Then we drive on...
Now, I have a responsibility
That makes me feel humility,
And integrity
At this point I should mention the power of my travel ca-ard!
Ho Ho HO!

Morris who has been quietly tapping his foot in rhythm to the music now drops his magazine, puts his whistle to his mouth, blowing hard like a madly out of kilter Peter Allen. He and Alice engage in a crazy tango-shimmey up and down the central isle. As Terry continues to provide backing music.

ALICE
(continues singing)
When the inspector...
When the inspector climbs aboard
My legs start shakin'
And a-quakin'
Whey they pile on,
I keep my smile on,
And then off we go again...
    (Alice and Morris bump backsides)
Turn around again
        (they turn)
And back again.
    (bump backsides again)

ALICE
(repeat chorus)
Whe-e-e-en the driver,
When the driver smiles at me
I go to Richmond.

TERRY
Or to Balwyn...

ALICE
Or to Burwood...

TERRY
Or to Hawthorn...

ALICE
Or East Melbourne

TERRY
Or to Deepdene

ALICE
Hartwell...

TERRY
Malvern...

ALICE
Geelong!

Suddenly Morris breaks off dancing.

MORRIS
Trams don't go to Geelong, Miss Cronin.

ALICE
Not yet they don't.

MORRIS
Oh- (right)

ALICE
(final statement, unaccompanied)
Because trams are the greatest, most intelligent, non-polluting form of transport ever invented.

Morris is forced to quietly agree.
Terry ends the interlude with a sequence of winding-up chords, then turns to Alice.

TERRY
What are you doing in 1984, then?

ALICE
Look, I liked my job, I liked what I was doing...

TERRY
Okay, you're happy, I'm happy, everybody's happy... Shake..
(holding out his hand)

Alice shakes all over.

ALICE
No thanks.

TERRY
Shake my hand!

Cautiously, Alice takes his hand. The shake.

TERRY
Just so long as we're friends.

TERRY
Hey, um, there's nobody in the back room is there?

He slowly puts his arm around Alice and gently starts leading her off towards the rear driver's door. Morris looks appalled.

MORRIS
I wouldn't go in there, if I were you, Miss Cronin. Your career with the MTGG might be over, but you don't want to ruin the rest of you life.

Prompted by Morris, Alice comes to her senses and throws Terry's arm off - just as the tram stops again and a somewhat inebriated Samantha staggers up the steps carrying a champagne cocktail.

SAM
Oh hullo, everybody!

Much general amusement at her return, and her condition.

SAM
Alice, darling, what a lovely surprise.
The same tram! How wonderful.
You know I've been walking all the way down Collins street and I still couldn't catch a cab.

TERRY
Yeah, well they won't take drunks, love.

Sam ignores the impertinence.

ALICE
How was Michael?

SAM
Wet, when I left him.

ALICE
What!

SAM
When he emerged for interval I tipped a champagne cocktail all over his Stafford Ellinson with the cut-away pockets.

ALICE

Gosh.

SAM

And you know, my dear, it was such a liberating experience that I ordered another one and did it again!
(laughs)

ALICE
(shocked but amused)

No! What did he do?

SAM

He just stood there and took it of course. Like the twerp that he is. Stood there like one of my stuffed eggplants. I just feel like this is the first night of the rest of my life. Without him.

ALICE

Didn't you stay for the show?

SAM

Before he even had time to recover I turned on my heel and walked out. I was so happy I ordered another cocktail and took it with me. Now I'm going home to take all my clothes off and leap naked into the swimming pool. And I simply don't care who sees me.

TERRY
(from down the back)

Mind if I come?

SAM

Ah, carrot-top, darling. Where's that lovely plastic puppie wuppie of yours?

TERRY
(disgusted)

Plastic!

SAM
I'm sorry, darling, I didn't mean plastic in the derogatory sense.

TERRY
The what sense?

Sam starts trying to whistle up the dog.

SAM
Bozo - here boy...has anyone seen a blind puppy?
(giggles, looking under seats)
Oh dear-
(straightening up, but still wobbly on her feet)
I feel quite a teenzy weensy bit dizzy

Sam looks around for something to steady her.

SAM
Is there a little spotty for a little botty?

She attempts to slide in next to someone. But there's hardly enough room so she keeps on sliding and ends up on the floor. Laughs at her predicament.

SAM
(from the floor)
Narrak avenue, thank you Alice, darling.

ALICE
That's another dollar ten thanks.

SAM
A dollar ten!
(rummaging in her Oroton handbag)
Just as well I didn't pour another glass over his head...
(chuckling)
Do you know what the Melbourne Theatre Company will symbolize for me from now on?

Alice takes her money, punches and hands her a travel card.

ALICE
No.

SAM
The end.

ALICE
Pardon?

SAM
The end of five years of being buried in Balwyn. I thought if I don't make a move now I'll be stuck there, just as everyone's moving to Noosa. Or Sanctuary Cove.

TERRY
Hey, lady, if I lived in Balwyn with a swimming pool, I wouldn't complain.

SAM
Oh, but you've got so much spark about you, carrot top! You and Alice both.

Alice and Terry share a look. Samantha hits on a bright idea.

SAM

Why don't we have a little party!? A few drinkies and a nude swim? I'll pop down to the four seven eleven and pick up some savouries...Michael always has plenty of booze...
    (turning to the rest of the passengers)
I'm sure he'd love to meet you all when he gets home. Ours is the double storey cream brick veneer at the top of the hill. With the two lions guarding the driveway...

General amusement at the prospect of going there spreads through the tram. Only Morris, who seems to have nodded off to sleep, remains unexcited.
Sam revels in the general enthusiasm.

SAM

Oh how thrilling!

But Terry throws a spanner in the works.

TERRY

Sorry,
    (putting a possessive arm around her)
Alice is coming to my party, Mrs. Hart-Byrne.

Alice throws his arm off.

ALICE
    (adamant.)
No I'm not.

SAM
    (conceding)
Well, yes of course, Balwyn is the pits, isn't it? No one with any spark would want to go there.

ALICE

I wouldn't mind a swim. After a hot shift like this.

TERRY
(sparking off the 'hot' part of that)
What? Naked?

SAM
Perhaps you'd better wear some togs. The Mont-Stephens next door may be merchant bankers but they're not above peeking through the fence when I sunbathe.

As if out of nowhere, Sam's mood plummets just as suddenly as it rose up at the thought of an impromptu party.

SAM
(almost spitting it out)
He's just so passionless!!!
We only did it once a week. Sunday morning. About as exciting as going to church.

TERRY
See how long you last without his bankcard, love.

ALICE
She's making a very important decision, haven't you ever left anyone you cared about?

Terry stares at her for a moment. Holding the attention. Then looks down, hurt, shrugs.

TERRY
(melodramatically)
Not until now...

He turns and walks away. Sam leans in to a fellow passenger. Speaking confidentially...

SAM
Chap back there said it was better than the national average. I suppose one must be grateful for small mercies...

Down the other end of the tram Terry is gently strumming his banjo again, quietly putting out 'a love gone wrong' sort of sound...Expressing his emotions through music.

The tram stops and Nigel and Cathy get back on. Nigel is totally caught up in his own brilliant insight. Yet another one.

> **NIGEL**
> The difference between film and television is the difference...
> (searching for the right word)
> between molecular change and atomic change. In other words: the difference between chemistry and physics. Video is pure product because it exists only as it is being transmitted. The chemistry of film on the other hand is tangible. You can look at it by holding it up to the light.

Nigel forms a rectangular film frame with four fingers - the classic 'director' pose. Then moves his 'camera' to frame Cathy in close up. She squirms away from the focus.

> **NIGEL**
> That's why I prefer film. It's real. It has a existence separate from electronics...

> **CATHY**
> You'd rather make a film than have a kid, wouldn't you, Nigel?

> **NIGEL**
> Sure I wanted to have kids, Cathy, but I wanted to have them in a 'stable' situation.

> **CATHY**
> Stable! The only stable part of you Nigel is the part that was left after the horse bolted.

NIGEL
Your mother never liked me.

CATHY
(sighs audibly)
Here we go again.

NIGEL
You don't trust me.

CATHY
I'm taking you home aren't I!

He can't deny it. Silence for a moment. Cathy is sorry that she yelled at him

CATHY
Look, Nigel, we've had a reasonably pleasant half an hour having a drink together, let's not spoil it by getting personal.

NIGEL
Personal!?

Terry has been getting bored again and decides to cause some mischief to jolly things along.

TERRY
Hey I really like the way your girlfriend moves, mind if I have a dance with her?

CATHY
Excuse me!

NIGEL
(flummoxed)
What?

TERRY
She a goer, then, eh?

CATHY
You can ask me if you've got any questions!

Terry's eyes light up at her resistance.

TERRY
Oh you are be-au-ti-full!

CATHY
God!

Cathy picks up her bag and moves down the back of the tram.
Terry quickly follows...followed by Nigel.

TERRY
I like it when you get all sultry.

Nigel manages to insert himself defensively between Cathy and Terry. Shirt fronting him.

NIGEL
Look, mate...

TERRY
(concentrating only on Cathy)
...makes you really attractive.

Cathy GROANS.

NIGEL
Mate, I wouldn't...I wouldn't flirt with her if I was you. I just don't think she's interested.

Terry swings around and pulls Nigel into a bear hug.

TERRY
That's alright, cause I'm interested in you too.

Nigel manages to shrug Terry off. Effectively pushing him away. Terry laughs.

NIGEL
(almost pleading)
Look, we've only got a few minutes, mate, and we'd like to have a quiet talk, okay?

TERRY
Mind if I listen in?
(obviously not going anywhere)

CATHY
(finally really angry)
Yeah, so just piss off!!

Nigel lets out a vicious yell and adopts a defensive Kung-Fu posture.

                    NIGEL
              (pumping his fists back
               and forth vicisiously)
        Ha! Ha! Ha! Ha! Ha!

His hands are like steel claws pointed straight at Terry.
Continues pumping his arms back and forth several
times, threatening.

                    NIGEL
        I don't want to hurt you.

Terry swings round, looking quizzical, immediately
grabs one of Nigel's hands and starts twisting his
fingers up backwards. Nigel's aggressive martial arts
posture just crumbles.

As Nigel groans in agony...

                    TERRY
        I'm only trying to be friendly.

Nigel collapses to his knees.

CATHY
(explodes)
Forgodsake why don't you just go away.

Terry lets go and leaves Nigel bowed over on the floor, trying to shake some blood back into his hands.

NIGEL

Sheeeah!

TERRY
OK, OK, I' not going to be heavy about it. You're not heavy about it - I'm not heavy about it. No hassles, right?

NIGEL
(scrambling to his feet)
No hassles.

TERRY
I just felt... you know... really attracted to you. How many people feel really attracted and never say it? I don't believe in holding back.
(to Nigel)
Isn't that right, killer?

NIGEL
(nodding, abject)
No hassles.

TERRY
But, if you don't want me to hang around, just stay so, and I'll mosey along...

CATHY
We don't want you to hang around - how many bloody times do we have to say it!

TERRY
(swings around to face her)
OK. But you don't know what you're missing out on.

CATHY
(not taking any shit)
I've got a fair idea.

NIGEL
(warning)

Cathy-

CATHY

What!

NIGEL

He's going.

CATHY

Good!

TERRY
(holding out his hand to Cathy)

Shake.

Cathy refuses to have anything more to do with Terry.
Folds her arms defiantly.

Nigel is nodding at her, encouraging her to take Terry's hand.

NIGEL
He won't go otherwise.

TERRY
I won't go otherwise.

Cathy just turns away.

NIGEL
(still urging)
Cathy -

CATHY
What!?

TERRY
Shake.

CATHY
Look, you shake his bloody hand. Just leave me out of it.

She gathers up her bag and pointedly moves down the other end of the tram. Wanting nothing more to do with either of them.

So Terry turns to Nigel. Holding out his hand.

TERRY
Shake.

                    NIGEL
>   Shake.

Very tentatively Nigel takes Terry's hand and Terry again applies the vice-like grip. He keeps pumping away long after Nigel would have preferred to withdraw.

Nigel's whole arm seems to go limp from the elbow.

                    TERRY
>   They say you can tell a man's personality by his handshake.

Nigel nods, finds himself unable to disagree.

TERRY
Not much to you is there tiger.

And Terry finally lets go.
Nigel shakes out his arm to get the blood moving again.

NIGEL
Sheeah! Man this is so Melbourne.
I mean, it's just so typical.

And makes his way back down towards Cathy.

CATHY
Coward.

NIGEL
Cathy, you've got to humour them or it could turn ugly.

CATHY
I can't stand it Nigel, I just can't stand it anymore.

NIGEL

What?

CATHY
All this interpersonal guerilla warfare.
It's ugly, I hate it.

Behind her Terry starts making GORILLA NOISES, scratching his ribs, curling his hands up.

NIGEL
The only dark cloud on tonight's horizon is your mother.

Cathy makes an audible SIGH. Here we go again.

NIGEL
If she hadn't blocked so much we might have had a chance back there.

CATHY
She's mellowed, alright?

NIGEL
She never read my poetry.

CATHY
Nigel, millions of people never read your poetry.

Nigel takes out a slip of paper.

NIGEL
I wrote this poem...my first important sonnet...
(reads)
Oh Muckdonalds - why am I always looking at your children's playgrounds through barbed wire?

CATHY
That's quite a metaphor.

NIGEL
I'm dedicating this to Derryn...
(goes to read on)

CATHY
Darryl.

NIGEL
Darryl.

CATHY
Look, Nigel, I don't care whether you come home or not. You wanted to see your son, it's up to you.

Alice is hovering, waiting to get their tickets. Still on duty despite being sacked. At least until the final depot.

NIGEL
Well I'm here aren't I?

Cathy shows Alice her pension card, hands over money.

CATHY
Pensioner concession, thanks.

Nigel fumbles in his pockets, uncertain.

NIGEL
Oh, ahm...the pizza sort of cleaned me out.

Cathy gives another two dollars to Alice.

CATHY
And one adult. Using the term loosely.

Alice punches and gives her two tickets with change. Goes back to dusting the tram. Cleaning the windows, polishing people's shoes, keeping herself busy.

NIGEL
I mean, we're all trapped by life, like...we're trapped by this tram. You know what I mean? Like in Bunuel's *Exterminating Angel*
(waits)
We're all trapped aren't we? Don't you think?
Alive... but for how long?

Down the other end of the tram Terry starts a slow hand clap.

TERRY
We've got an artist on board.

NIGEL
Yes and there's very few of us left. I mean,
(looking around/passionate)
does anybody here know what it takes to be an artist!?

Nigel waits for a response.

NIGEL
Hmm? Well? Does anybody here have any idea of the kind of commitment that involves!? The passion, the struggle for insight? I mean, what do you feel when you look up at the stars at night? Huh?

CATHY
(warning)
Nigel-

But, having recently been physically humiliated by Terry, Nigel is on a roll. He addresses the whole tram, like a life coach, or a priest in his pulpit.

NIGEL
Are they just dots in the sky - ? Or does some overwhelming primal fear take over? Of how small and insignificant we really are. I mean, here we are man, we're just sparks of consciousness - a brief candle burning for a nano-second of cosmic time.
  (as if discovering this insight at this moment)
We're here so that the universe can become conscious of itself!
    (a pause he looks around
      as if waking up
      and then out the window)
I mean look up at the stars - just crane your heads through the window and look up. Take a good, hard squizz, go on…See? See?

Nigel is urging them to look out and up. Terry takes a cursory peek through the glass door.

TERRY
It's cloudy.

NIGEL
What?

TERRY
It's cloudy. You can't see any stars.

NIGEL
(suddenly deflated)
Oh - of course, this is Melbourne. Isn't it?
You poor saps just don't get a chance, do you?
No wonder you all think you're so significant down here. You - have – no - idea.

The tram is now a few stops past where Danny got chucked off so unceremoniously on the way in. Terry has taken up his banjo again and starts threading his way towards Alice, serenading her with a popular love song. Coming on strong.

Consequently, when the tram stops he fails to notice an enraged Danny stagger back on, brandishing a rolled up newspaper. He reeks of sweet sherry and is roaring like a demon, seething with revenge.

> **DANNY**
> Hey! Remember me? Eh? Son?

Danny whacks Terry in the back of the head. Terry immediately swings round, defensive. Arms protecting his head.

> **TERRY**
> Careful of the instrument, mate.
> (handing the banjo to a passenger)
> Look after this for me will you, mate.

Danny picks up one of Terry's legs forcing him to hop as he pulls him towards the door. Pandemonium breaks out. The women and Nigel screaming.

> **DANNY**
> You're getting off. Bastard.

> **TERRY**
> (hopping along, trying to balance, but not really threatened)
> Hey, derro -

> **DANNY**
> Very funny wasn't it. Picking on an old pensioner.

TERRY
Hey, no look, no - I'd have a go at the driver, mate, if I was you... the way he just took off like that, Eh ? Back there...I tried to tell him. I said stop, the old codger wants to get back on.

DANNY
You're OFF!!

TERRY
Give me me foot back.

DANNY
You're finished shithead, you're outta here...

The tram stops, the door opens and Danny starts trying to ram Terry out through it. Terry spreads his arms and legs across the open doorway, resisting. Hanging there like a gothic spider. No way can Danny push him out.

Up the other end of the tram Nigel is in a panic. Turns to people around him.

NIGEL
Somebody's got to DO something!

And starts taking photos of himself.

CATHY
Stop it Nigel, you'll go blind.

NIGEL
(snapping away)
I just want to get a record of my emotional reaction.

Danny continues to beat Terry with his newspaper and tries to shove him out through the open door. Alice hovers behind Danny, but feels powerless to intervene. She turns to a still sleeping Morris Stanley and tries to shake him awake. But Morris just snores on through it all. Dead asleep behind his *True Crime* magazine.

DANNY
Bloody young punk bastard, mongrel animal. I'll *KILL* you!!

This is getting all a bit much for Terry who easily swivels around Danny, and secures himself back inside the tram. He soon shakes his foot free and immediately twists Danny's arm up behind his back. Danny YELPS in pain.

TERRY
Are you thick or what? It was the bloody driver, I tell you. You just can't trust them.

Nigel is looking for more dramatic shots. Framing a fellow passenger now in the foreground and urging them to act.

NIGEL
Could you like, do something?
(takes a shot)
More fear... could you do that again, but look a bit more afraid? I think the light was a bit too contrasty.

While Terry and Danny continue their strange dance around each other.

DANNY
You're history numbskull !!!

With a superhuman effort, born of anger and humiliation, Danny manages to wrench himself free of the arm lock and soon grips Terry in a rather demeaning half-nelson.

Samantha decides something official has to be done, she strides up to Morris, still slumped asleep over his trashy crime magazine. She grabs his hearing aid and speaks directly into it.

SAM
Testing one, two, three...

Morris snaps awake. Suddenly bewildered.

MORRIS
Wha....!

SAM
Excuse me, Inspector, but there is an atrocity being committed...
(aboard this tram)

Morris tugs his hearing aid back in disgust. Perplexed as to what this stupid woman is on about now.

MORRIS
Atrocity!? What atrocity!?

And then it hits him - literally, as Terry sling-shots Danny into Morris, who in turn barrels into Samantha, knocking the three of them flying.

TERRY
You've flipped your lid you stupid old derro.

                              DANNY
                      (more insults from Terry)
            STUPID!

Morris struggles to his feet, appalled. Sam appeals
directly to him.

                               SAM
            Can't you see what they're doing!?

Morris nervously reaches for his whistle, puts it to his
mouth and blows hard, but the damn thing doesn't
seem to work. He blows and blows but no whistle
comes out. The pea seems stuck.

                              TERRY
            Okay, okay, you're not stupid, you're a genius,
            fercrissake. I thought the exercise would do you good.

Danny converts the rear naked choke into a headlock
and slams Terry into the rear driver's door. There's a
sickening thud. Terry twists back to face Danny,
wobbling his head, holding it where it hurts, and
quickly draws a knife.

                              TERRY
            Right! That does it!

There's a shocked intake of breath all round as he
brandishes the knife out towards Danny and anyone
else prepared to try it on.

                              DANNY
                      (putting his hands out in front, protectively,
                              suddenly contrite)
            Now listen, mate.

People give Terry a wide berth, Danny, terrified, is backing away.

TERRY
No, you listen for a change, you mangey old coot.

Morris has finally shaken the pea loose in his whistle and gives it a good BLAST. Things come to a halt as Morris marches straight up to Terry.

MORRIS
I am an official representative of the Melbourne Metropolitan Tramways Board and I'm ordering you to sheaf that knife at once.

TERRY
(parrying the knife out towards Morris, threatening, twirling it towards his nose)
Ordering me to what?

Morris takes a tentative step back. But remains firm.

MORRIS
Alright, alright, I'm...strenuously urging you to...to...
(starting to crumble)

TERRY
To what?

Terry points the knife straight up under Morris's chin.

MORRIS
(shaking)
To...to...p p p put the...I'm warmly encouraging you to, to...

TERRY
(screaming into his face)
ENCOURAGING!

MORRIS
Pleading...begging...I'm, I'm reasonably firm about it.

TERRY
Get down on your knees and bark like a dog.

MORRIS
Wha...? Now listen...

TERRY
Go on, bark, dog!

MORRIS
This wasn't in the script.
TERRY
(thrashing out with the knife in all directions)
You wanna get cut!

Morris immediately drops to his knees and starts barking.

MORRIS
Woof, woof, woof.

TERRY
Good, good, now we understand each other, dog to man right?

MORRIS
Sir, I am trying to see it from your point of view.

TERRY
Bark when you talk to me, dog.

MORRIS
Woof, woof, woof.

ALICE
Terry, you'll cost me my job.

TERRY
You've already lost it, haven't you?

DANNY
Ah, what do punks care about the working class!
(straight at Terry)
I fought in the streets for your right to play video ping pong. Conscientious objectors went underground to save twerps like you from the Cambodian jungle.

Morris takes some courage from Danny's defiant stand. He points to the war ribbons and medals on his trench coat.

MORRIS
You see that badge! You know what that badge means?

TERRY
Bark!

MORRIS
Woof. woof.

DANNY
(running straight on)
Signed petitions and got stomped on by police horses and for what? Eh? So that the New Wave can put a safety pin in its earhole.
(pointing at Terry's safety pin)
You're the swine generation, you know that?

TERRY
(holding the knife up vertically)
Sit on that and swivel, commo.

DANNY
Cawd, the bands you listen to nowadays have got about as much musical talent as the hordes of Genghis Khan.

MORRIS
(trying to restrain Danny)
Please don't antagonize him.

DANNY & TERRY
(shouting together at him)
SHUT UP!

MORRIS
Woof. Woof.

ALICE
Put it down, Terry!

TERRY
(rounding on Danny - who backs off a little)
So you reckon you fought for us, do you, Tiger?
And what did it amount to, eh?
Is there anymore understanding in this world?
Do you know why I dress like this?

DANNY
I've got a fair idea.

TERRY
Well you're wrong! It's because I want to be noticed, see, when I walk down the street I want people to see *me*, Terry, and when they stop and stare I say:
(rounding on a passenger)
"What are you lookin' at dead head?!"
(laughs)

Morris takes the opportunity of Terry swinging round to start yapping at his heels, going overboard with the dog impersonation. Starting to seriously crack up...

Terry quickly rebalances to confront Morris head, on menacing him with the knife. Morris quickly retreats on all fours yelping like a hurt puppy.

SAM
Isn't it marvelous that people can air their differences like this in public?

Morris lifts up to kneeling in front of Terry and puts a hand out defensively, suddenly firm and seeking to finally wrest control.

MORRIS

Now listen, just p p p put the weapon down before you cut yourself. My grandmother got a stiff thumb from a knife like that.

Terry lunges at Morris again, who quickly YELPS like a wounded animal and retreats on all fours, seeking to hide under a seat. At last Alice plunges in, determined to stop this outbreak of anarchy on her tram.

ALICE

Put it down, Terry!

DANNY

Ya doomed, 'cause ya not organized!

ALICE
(rounding on him)

Shut-up!
Everybody just shut-up! And listen to me!

MORRIS
(clearly becoming slightly unhinged)
You're a good lad and you've got a bright future ahead of you...

ALICE
(screaming)
Just SHUDDUPP!!

Morris meekly defers to her clearly stronger personality. And much louder voice.

ALICE
(putting her hand out to take it)
Just stop being so bloody stupid and give me that knife.

TERRY
Will you come out with me?

ALICE
This is exactly the sort of incident that gives trams a bad name.

TERRY
I'll put it away if you say yes...

ALICE
You want to drive people off their own form of transport, is that what you want? Force everyone to buy a car? Consume petrol. Pollute the atmosphere.

DANNY
Yer talkin' to a brick wall, love, you have to be on "Countdown" before he'll listen to ya.

TERRY
Well ?
(holding out the knife tempting her)

MORRIS
Please say you'll go out with him, Miss Cronin. Think of the Melbourne Metropolitan Transport Board.

SAM
(disdainful)
Oh how awful...

ALICE
(firm, as if talking to a child)
Give it to me.

TERRY
(indicating Morris)
They'll throw the book at me.

MORRIS
I can assure you sir, there will be no further action taken.

ALICE
You hear that? Terry? No further action...

Terry thinks about it. But can he trust Morris?

TERRY
Say you'll go out with me.

ALICE
Maybe...

TERRY
Not good enough.
(rounding back on Morris)
Bark

MORRIS
Woof, woof, woof...
Forgodsake, Miss Cronin!!!

                    ALICE
Will I get my job back?

                    MORRIS
              (that maybe going a bit far)
    What?
                    ALICE
                    (adamant)
No job. No deal.

Terry menaces Morris. Forcing the issue. Morris backs down immediately.

                    MORRIS
Well, well, yes... Of course you will.
My word is my bond.
You can trust me implicitly...

                    ALICE
Trust you!?

                    MORRIS
I happen to be a grand wizard of the Hawthorn Masonic lodge.

Alice weighs that up for a moment.

                    ALICE
Alright, DAMNIT! Then, yes. I'll go out with you! Okay? Now give me the knife.

Terry grins, savouring the moment. Turns the knife around, handle safely pointed towards Alice. Then slowly gives it to her. Wraps her fingers around the handle and gently kisses her hand.

Morris, relieved, brushes the dirt off his trouser knees and jumps to his feet.

MORRIS
Well done, Miss Cronin!

He cautiously comes forward and tentative, takes the knife off Alice.

MORRIS
I'll take matters in hand now, thank you.

Suddenly contorting with rage, Morris rounds on Terry and slams him up against a pole near the doorway.

MORRIS
Right, you bloated filth!

Morris menaces Terry with the knife in one hand, raising it high above his head and almost chokes him with the other. Alice feels compelled to protest.

ALICE
You gave him your word!

MORRIS
I wouldn't give him the carrots out of my vomit if he was starving in the gutter!

MORRIS
(back to Terry)
In fact the only thing stopping me from ramming this into your fetid guts right now is the delicious thought of you stewing in Pentridge, 'till that pink hair turns yellow...or mauve...or whatever colour it really is.
(preparing to plunge the knife into him)
You aneurism!

Sam screams, Terry rears back and Alice intercepts Morris's lunge just in time, seizing the knife back, easily twisting it out of his hand. Morris looks around at her, suddenly empty handed, stunned.

MORRIS
But M...Miss Cronin...

ALICE

You said you wouldn't.

Terry slips in between them and grabs the knife back.

                      TERRY
Thank you Alice.
    (pushing Morris back against the pole)

In the next moment Danny comes up behind him and seizes the knife off Terry

                      DANNY
Thank you Terry.

...and grabbing Morris in a bear hug, Danny immediately holds the knife back up to the unfortunate ticket inspector's throat.

                      MORRIS
    (panicked/warning)
Ha! Ah! Now look here...

Danny drags Morris towards the rear of the tram. Holding the knife against his jugular.

                      DANNY
Get back! Get back!

                      MORRIS
Get back! Get back!

                      DANNY
I'll kill him!

                      MORRIS
He'll kill me.
    (swallows hard)

Could someone call a doctor, I... I suffer from a nervous complaint.
I ....can't stand the sight of blood.

DANNY
Don't move! Don't move!

MORRIS
Don't move! Don't move!
Miss Cronin help!

DANNY
Right. Now I'm hijacking this tram!

Sam faints. General pandemonium.

TERRY
Ah ya mad ya stupid old windbag.

MORRIS
Please, please don't antagonize him. Just treat him like a child.
> (rummaging through his pockets, locating, wallet, photos)

You see my wife, my family, my budgie, William,...they depend on me a lot.

Morris's wife looks like somebody who could easily have been in charge of a Nazi concentration camp.

DANNY
Disgusting. Put it away.

MORRIS
> (hastily doing so)

Sir, I'm completely at your disposal.

DANNY
Oh, are you just? Well that's real good. 'Cause I tell you what, mate - I got on this tram in the early part of the afternoon, well before the second at Flemington, with the simple intention of going straight home. For eight flaming hours I've been trying to get there, and I just can't take it anymore!

MORRIS
Your condition is firmly impressed on my mind. Your complaints will be taken up the right channels.

DANNY
Well that's very, very good. Because what I want you and Miss Cronin here to do is really very, very simple...

MORRIS
(relieved)
Oh...oh good. I, I feel I can speak for both us.
(nodding at Alice)

DANNY
I just want you to turn this tram around and take us all back to Mont Albert.

Morris sinks a little at the knees.

TERRY
Ah - ya mad ya stupid old goat!

DANNY
Yeah? Well, I'll you what. I'm not going to be pushed around anymore, see. I'm jack of the lot of it. And you want to know something for nothing? I'm not going to try to change society anymore, because its not bloody worth it. Why bother fixing a system that's totally stuffed. The only good thing you can do with Balwyn, love, is put a bloody bomb under it. I just want to massacre Malvern, trash Toorak, bugger-up Brighton, by kerrist, I'm going to take Mont Albert by stooooooorrrrmmmm!

MORRIS
(a stickler for the rules)
Well, you'll need a travel card.

DANNY
(contemptuous)
Travel card! I just about paid for me life with this ride, mate.

ALICE
Anyway, we can't turn round.

MORRIS
Miss Cronin, I'm giving the orders here.

ALICE
I can't do it.

DANNY
Yes you can.

MORRIS
Yes you can.

ALICE
No I can't.

DANNY
(like a child having a tantrum)
I want to go back!

ALICE
You can't go back.

DANNY
But I want to go back!

ALICE
But you can't go back

MORRIS/DANNY
Why NOT?!

ALICE
Because this is a tram. It doesn't *go* backwards.

DANNY
(almost weeping)
I just want to get home.

ALICE
We're already going to Mont Albert!!

DANNY
Wha..?

Danny looks blank. How can that be?
He glances out through a window, squinting at the passing landscape. Trying to find something familiar.

DANNY
Now don't try and confuse me, love, just turn the bloody tram around, 'cause we're not stopping till we crash through Box Hill.

Alice gives up, moving forward to talk to the driver.

ALICE
Alright, but it'll only take you back to the city.

DANNY
(completely confused)
Well how come I'm facing the same was I was facing when we were going the other way?

ALICE
(pointing at it)
Have a look at the destination roller...

Flummoxed, Danny cranes a head around to look. But of course it's impossible to see the destination roller from inside the tram.

DANNY
Where?

MORRIS
(pointing vaguely outside, distracting him)
There!

Seizing the opportunity of Danny's bewilderment, Morris lunges for the knife, Danny resists and they struggle clumsily over it

DANNY
Hey! Hey!

Morris is slapping Danny's knife-hand back against a hanging strap. Neither of them obviously have a clue how to fight. But they continue their inept struggle for possession of the weapon, putting all their limited strength into it.

Until finally, Danny hunches over, leaning into Morris, the knife hidden between their coats. Both wrestling for it until... there's a final push from Morris, and a loud GROAN from Danny, who slumps to the floor. Morris collapses down on top of him.

TERRY
Hey, now cut that out fellas...no bro-mancing allowed on trams.

Morris pulls back in horror, staggers to his feet, dropping the knife. He looks at his hands, they're smeared in a thick, red, gooey mess. Imitating Edvard Munch's "The Scream", Morris's 'blood' stained hands go to his hollow cheeks, he looks horrified by what he's done. Eyes widening. Automatically he steps back from 'the body', shaken with guilt. Automatically one hand now loosens his tie, smearing more red goo over his shirt. The other hand reaches to pull the cord to stop the tram. Danny remains 'dead' on the floor.

                    MORRIS
     (mumbling to himself, clearly demented)
I...I wonder if I took the chops out of the freezer...? We'll need some vegemite too, for the soup. And half a pound of butter. I'll pick them up on the way home. Thelma hasn't had her shots this week, either. I'll have to remind her about that...
                   (sudden primal yell)

They never told me the job would be like this!
>(tries to vomit, can't quite)

Oh god, there'll be headlines in the *Truth*.
Old photos of me will appear on television.
I've let the department down.
I'm sorry. I'm... so, so sorry!
>(breaks down, weeping)

Nigel sidles up to him, confidential. Offering a card.

NIGEL
Listen, I could give you the name of a good shrink...
You'll find his primal work very effective.

Morris hovers near the door, gazes at Nigel blankly,
then a sudden injection of pain.

MORRIS
Off. I want to get off!
>(obsessed with his blood stained hands)

Oh Kerrist! Won't somebody stop the tram!?

Alice pulls the cord again.

MORRIS
(muttering to himself)
I didn't mean to do it. Woof. Woof. He, he pushed me. Yes, it's all his fault. I, I just...I...he took the knife, he...he...

The tram finally stops and Morris staggers off. Holding his hands out in front of him, shaking them at the cars backing up, waiting for him to cross to the footpath. He walks with a strange limp, quite unhinged. Suddenly laughing manically.

Alice hangs in the doorway. Looking moderately concerned.

ALICE
Morris, Mr. Stanley... come back!

NIGEL
He reminds me of her mother.

CATHY
(warning)
Nigel...

NIGEL
(to a random passenger)
Why didn't you do something?

Samantha seems to recover from her faint.
While, down the back, Danny is crawling around on all fours quietly groaning. He looks at his own hands, also stained with the thick, red, gooey substance.

DANNY
He's bloody killed me the bugger.

SAM
Oh there's absolutely no need to worry. I've done a course in bandaging and animal husbandry at the Camberwell Leisure Centre.

Danny indicates Terry with a bloody finger. Red ooze falling onto the floor.

TERRY
(protesting)
Hang on -

DANNY
Bastard!

Danny quickly scoops up the knife from where Morris dropped it and lunges it straight into Terry's mid-section. Stabbing multiple times. Again, screams from Sam and Alice.

General pandemonium.

But Terry just hangs there, grinning broadly. Opening his arms widely, inviting Danny in. Talking the blows amazingly calmly. Danny continues to stab at Terry with no apparent effect.

Terry holds his palm up. Danny lunges the knife in, but the blade just disappears into the handle and bounces back out. It's a plastic toy knife.

Danny plunges it into his own palm and watches the blade disappear and reappear again.

DANNY
What? It's a bloody trick knife! Ha!

The relief is palpable and instantaneous. Suddenly Danny and Terry are laughing. Danny shows off, plunging the blade into the side of his head.

                    DANNY
    Der...

Then Danny suddenly remembers his stomach. Sniffs his fingers and opens his shirt to reveal a smashed meat pie and tomato sauce.

                    DANNY
    Me lunch. The bastard's stabbed me lunch!

                    TERRY
    Thought yer blood was worth bottlin' did ya, mate?

                    ALICE
    (firmly but sadly to Terry)
    I'll never forgive you for this.

And goes about cleaning up the mess left under the seat by the smashed pie.

TERRY
It was only a joke fercrissake.

Danny is holding out what's left of his pie, appealing to the tram generally.

DANNY
Who's going to pay for this then? Eh?

TERRY
You got tomato sauce all over me nice clean knife.

DANNY
I thought I was dead, you bastard.
"Inspector knife's gentleman between residences" - not the sort of poetry I had in mind for my obituary.

Meanwhile, up the other end of the tram, distraught by all that's just happened, Nigel is having an existential crisis.

NIGEL
What am I doing here?

CATHY
Nigel...

NIGEL
What's happening to my head?

CATHY
Please try and remain calm.

NIGEL
I'm on a Melbourne tram going back to visit your mother.

CATHY
You invited yourself. I don't care what you do.

NIGEL
I was coming round to the idea that I could actually relate to you again.

CATHY

How thrilling for you.

NIGEL

Cathy...

CATHY

I don't want to discuss it Nigel. It's over. It was over a long time ago.

NIGEL

Oh well, let's just lapse back into our usual silence again.

There's a silence. The tram rattles on. Nigel waits. He starts pacing, up and down. Clearly distressed.

NIGEL

It's just... It's just...

CATHY

Look, my mother will grow on you, alright?

NIGEL
She grows on me like a rare skin disease. Probably shingles.

CATHY
(gives up)
Oh!

NIGEL
Every time I see her I smell... napalm.

CATHY
Do you want to meet your son, or what?

Clearly he does. But...

NIGEL
She hates me.

CATHY
She's mellowed.

NIGEL
She has a voodoo doll of me, I know she sticks pins in it.

CATHY
Your imagination is bad for you.

NIGEL
Pressure is your art form, isn't it Cathy?

CATHY
(appealing to the heavens)
Oh God!

NIGEL
Alright, then, fine. Fine!
I'll just pull the cord and go.

CATHY
(peremptory)
Good.

NIGEL
What?

CATHY
Good-bye.

Nigel is set back. He didn't expect the bum's rush.

NIGEL
Good- (bye)? That's it? Finito la musica?

CATHY
(waving him off)
Ta Ta...

NIGEL
(hurt)
I'll probably never see you again.

CATHY
Can I have that in writing?

Nigel is gobsmacked. He just hangs there. Mouth open. Jaw slack.

NIGEL
You're serious!?

CATHY
You promised me that last time and I didn't believe you then, either.
It was doomed to start with.

NIGEL
Doomed?

CATHY
Doomed.

NIGEL
Why isn't this traumatic for you?

CATHY
I'll send you an invoice for my services.

NIGEL
You're what? You're saying...

CATHY
Yes, escort services. That's what I do. I escorted you to a cup of coffee.

NIGEL
That kind of cheap joke, hurts, Cathy.

CATHY
Who's joking?

NIGEL
I think you mean it.

Nigel just hangs there, nodding, depressed. Wounded.

NIGEL
Whatever happened to enlightenment?

CATHY
Drain your brain, Nigel, that's your en-lighten-ment.

NIGEL
Why, why won't you see how attracted I am to you.

CATHY
You're boring.

NIGEL
(genuinely shocked/disbelieving/
nodding open mouthed)

What?
I'm...

CATHY
(stifling a yawn)
You're boring. Go away.

She moves off up the other end of the tram.

Nigel just hangs there for a moment. He can't believe it.

After a few moments he moves after her.

NIGEL
I'm not boring. I don't bore people.

CATHY
How do you know?

NIGEL
I've asked them!

CATHY
I rest my case.

NIGEL
I don't bore my shrink.

CATHY
That's cause you *pay* him to listen to you.
You want me to stand here and listen. You pay me.

NIGEL
You're the mother of my only child. We're practically related.

CATHY
And never got a cent for it.

DANNY
You give it to him love!

NIGEL
(annoyed people are listening in)
For a moment there it was really good to see you, Cathy. You know that? Half and hour ago I was moderately happy.

CATHY
I'll be happy as soon as you're off the tram.

TERRY
(sending them up)

Ooooh.

Alice hits Terry in the ribs with the end of her feather duster. It hurts. It was meant to. He settles down, like everyone, waiting for Nigel and Cathy's dramatic separation to play out.

NIGEL

Look at me. I mean look at me.

DANNY

Do we have to?

NIGEL

35 years old and I still can't properly relax.
I still hover on the brink of my brilliant career.

CATHY

Yes, I've finally realized there is a film script in you Nigel. Because you're a walking tragedy!

NIGEL
(pulling the cord)

Okay, okay, I get the message. No need to embellish it with sarcasm. I'll see myself out.

CATHY

Good.

NIGEL

I said, "I'm going."

CATHY

What a relief.

NIGEL

What?

CATHY

Good-bye.

NIGEL

Well stuff it, Cathy!

The tram stops and Nigel hovers in the doorway on the brink of walking out of Cathy and his newly discovered but still unseen son forever.

CATHY

And stuff you!

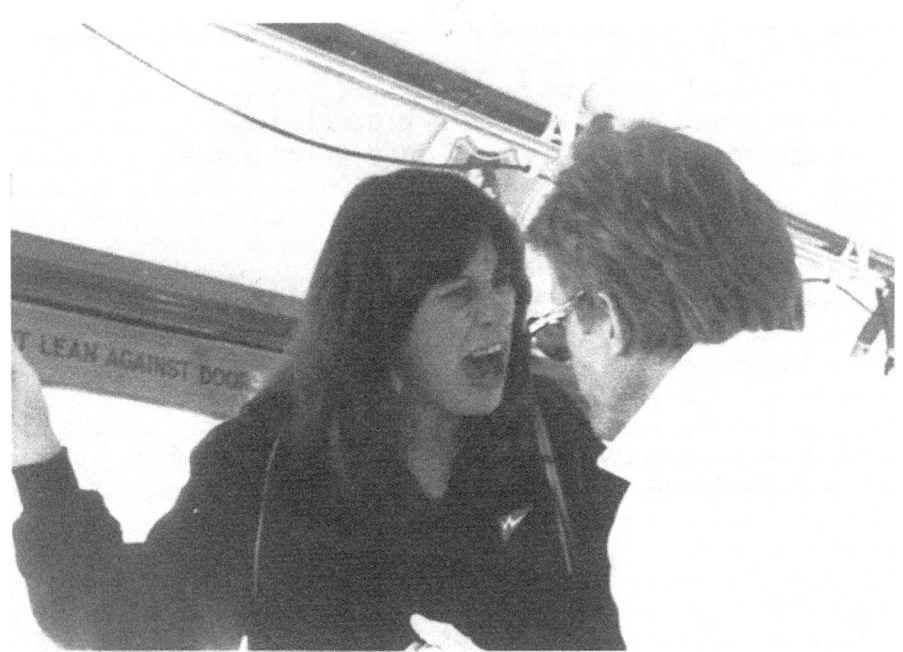

NIGEL
And stuff Melbourne. And stuff your mother!

CATHY
How dare you talk about my mother like that in public.

NIGEL
(from the doorway)
I gave you the best years of my life!!

CATHY
(screaming back)
Wan-ker.
(she makes a rude gesture towards him)

NIGEL
(backing out onto the street,
screaming back up at her from the step)
Nothing but Blood! Sweat! and Tears!!

Nigel swings around to fully disembark and walks straight into the capacious arms of Sgt Warren Wilkinson and Const. Cyril Foster. Who immediately sweep him back on board, ahead of them as they come on.

CYRIL
Just get back inside, son.

NIGEL
What?

WARREN
Step back inside, please...

NIGEL
What is this?

The cops continue to push Nigel back on board ahead of them. Warren speaks into the radio clipped to his shirt collar.

WARREN
Copy that D24. We're on board now.

Cyril pulls the cord to start the tram and it moves on again.

CYRIL
We've just had a report about blood on this tram.

NIGEL
What!?

WARREN
Yellow cab, five minutes ago, radio'd D24 with reports of a disturbance.

NIGEL
Disturbance?

CYRIL
Involving grievous bodily harm.

NIGEL
I might have yelled a little.
We didn't even get to the bodily part of it.

WARREN
That's what they all say.

Alice comes up, trying to settle the confusion.

ALICE
But officer it wasn't a real murder - it, it was only his lunch that got stabbed.

WARREN
Who's lunch got murdered?

ALICE
The old man who thought he was dead. It was only a pie and sauce.

WARREN
Who thought who was dead?

CYRIL
What was only a pie and sauce?
ALICE
His lunch!
(of course)

Warren and Cyril share a knowing look.

WARREN
Fruitcakes.
CYRIL
And not even a full moon, senior.

ALICE
But Mr. Stanley...the inspector. He's gone off into the night. He thinks he did it.

WARREN
Did what?

ALICE
The stabbing.

Warren and Cyril share another look.

WARREN
Looks like we'll just have to take them one at a time, Cyril.

CYRIL
Right, senior.

ALICE
But you've got to find him, he was in a terrible state. I'm afraid he could do anything. He was like shell shocked or something.

WARREN
(turning to Alice as the only other authority on board)
Now let's be clear about this. Were there or were there not threats of violence uttered?

NIGEL
Christ, officer, I only said I'd *like* to kill her.

CYRIL
Kill who?

NIGEL
(indicating Cathy)
Her mother! She'd like to kill me!

WARREN
And where's the said woman, now, son?

NIGEL
I don't know, I haven't laid eyes on her for over six years.

DANNY
And where's your helicopter?

Cyril swings round to confront Danny. More trouble looming...

CYRIL
If you don't mind, sir. We're conducting a serious investigation here.

DANNY
Makes more noise than a sick chook in a cyclone.

Warren indicates Nigel to Cyril.

WARREN
Put the cuffs on this one, constable.

CYRIL
Right you are, senior.

Cyril comes forward and handcuffs Nigel to the hand rail.

NIGEL
What? What is this? What have I done?
(appealing to her for help)
Cathy?

Danny starts prancing around the back of the tram.

DANNY
Hands up, hands up, you're all under arrest.

NIGEL
Listen, I'm Nigel Davidson, you know?
Nigel Davidson Productions...
(as if they should know)
I've been on Channel Ten. You must've heard of me.
(searching for a business card with his free hand)

But the cops are distracted by Danny who continues to prance around like he's got nothing left to lose

DANNY
Hands up. Hands up. You're all guilty. You all stood by and let it happen.

But Danny's raised arms only reveal all the watches strapped there.
Cyril and Warren slowly approach him and take an arm each,
examining what are obviously pretty dodgy goods.

WARREN
Would you mind telling me how you can into possession of the said watches I asked at...

Cyril checks his watch.

CYRIL
10.08 pm, Senior.

Warren sighs, rolls his eyes, it's as if he's still got to train him.

WARREN
The evidence, constable. Come on son, keep your wits about you.

The penny drops.

CYRIL
Oh right...sorry Senior. You asked at...
  (reading the time up and down Danny's arms)
At... 10.09, 10.11, 10.20, 12.18, 9.32 and 7.45 am. Sir. According to the evidence.

WARREN
Very good Cyril.
  (noting the times down)

CYRIL
  (pleased)
Thank you senior.

DANNY
Look, me brother-in-law's a jeweler in Richmond, fercrissake.

WARREN
And not a very kosher one either, by the sound of it, pal. Selling watches that slow, it's almost criminal.

CYRIL
And you can drop the blasphemy unless you want it added to the list of charges.

DANNY
What list of charges?

WARREN
Receiving, disturbing the peace, selling stolen goods, exposing yourself. You're under arrest, pal.

DANNY
You can't do this to me. I'm a full member of the Duke of Edinburgh trust.

The cops get a whiff of Danny for the first time, fanning the air between them.

CYRIL
You're full alright, whether you remember is another matter entirely.

Warren and Cyril think that's a huge joke, slap their sides. Laughing.

SAM
And officer, he's not the only one.

Standing next to her, Terry fans the air as well. Reacting to *her* fumes.

TERRY
You can say that again.

Sam, who has been slowly sipping her stolen cocktail from the MTC is inebriated enough now to throw herself into the deep end - just for the hell of it. Hoping perhaps, the scandal will someway reflect badly on Michael.

SAM
I'm one too. I'm terribly, frightfully, awfully, dreadfully guilty. I poured two champagne cocktails all over my husband's receding hairline and then I went and stole another glass from a leading Melbourne theatre company and did it again. I demand to be taken into custody.

                    WARREN
        Yes, yes, Madam. All in good time.
                  (back to Danny)
        Now what's all this business about a stabbing?

Sam looks disappointed that they're not taking her
seriously. Danny remains on his high moral horse.

                    DANNY
        It's not me you should be asking it's that ginger
        headed thug skulking down the back.

With fading eyesight, Danny tries to point out Terry
who is quietly managing to fade into the background.

                    CYRIL
        We'd like to start with you sir, if you don't mind.

                    DANNY
        He stole a blind dog and wouldn't give me me tranny
        back.
                  (indicating a passenger)
        And that lousey bugger wouldn't buy a watch off me.

                    WARREN
                  (correcting)
        Stolen watch.

Warren sighs and nods at Cyril to continue and he
proceeds to put another pair of cuffs on Danny and
attaches him to Samantha.

                    SAM
                  (not sure this is a good idea)
        Oh...

CYRIL
I'm taking these arms in evidence to be used against you.

DANNY
I never wanted to come on this damn fool trip anyway! It's all his fault.
    (indicating Terry)
Geeze constable. I just wanted to go back to Mont Albert.

CYRIL
    (sudden explosion)
You're not going anywhere until we've bashed a statement out of you!

WARREN
    (warning)
Constable!

CYRIL
Oh, sorry, senior, yes, yes, until we...take you back to the station where we...will...

WARREN
...encourage...

CYRIL
...encourage you to make...

WARREN
...a statement outlining your guilt.

DANNY
But I've stopped making statements. I told them before. I've called it quits politically. This pack of drongos isn't *worth* saving. They've lost my respect completely.

WARREN
What are you some kind of socialist or something?

SAM
(this is getting worse)
Oh no!

DANNY
When I said "Bomb Balwyn" I didn't mean "bomb" literally.

Warren and Cyril rear back, horrified.

WARREN/CYRIL
(together/shock)
BOMB!!!

DANNY
It was more like a figure of speech, you know. Alliteration...
Like 'B' for "Bugger up", or 'B' for briefcase...

WARREN/CYRIL
BRIEFCASE!!!

Together Warren and Cyril swing around and freeze on seeing Nigel handcuffed to the hand rail, still holding his...briefcase. Just hanging there, looking blank.

WARREN
(from as far back as he can get)
Clear the forward saloon.

CYRIL

Ah, Warren...

WARREN
(urging, almost pushing him forward)
Quickly Cyril. Procedure, son.

CYRIL

Why do I always have to do the bombs?

WARREN

You see that stripe!
(indicating his rank)

CYRIL
(reluctantly/resigned)
Oh alright...

Cyril almost tip-toes forward.

> **CYRIL**
> Everybody just stay calm...please remain perfectly still, as the slightest movement could trigger a massive explosion. Do not panic, although this is an extreme emergency and your lives are all in considerable danger.

Everybody around Nigel seems to hang back from him, isolating him into the spotlight even further. He's still hanging by the handcuffs and trying, not very successfully, to push his briefcase out the window or under a nearby seat. Certainly, nobody wants to take it.

As Cyril continues to inch his way towards Nigel he puts his hands out defensively, almost expecting a blast at any time.

> **CYRIL**
> N, n, now, son, just take it easy, okay, remain perfectly still, and breathe as gently as you can - okay - just breath normally.

Nigel takes big lungfulls of air, trying to follow orders, trying to calm his natural anxiety at the best of times let alone a real crisis like this.

> **CYRIL**
> (encouraging)
> - N, n, now I'll mention this co-operation to the magistrate - if you can just tell us as gently as you can ...what is in the briefcase?

> **NIGEL**
> What!?

Nigel panics, drops the briefcase. It "explodes" open.

Warren and Cyril SCREAM and UTTER EXPLETIVES as they hit the deck, covering their heads with their hands. For extra protection Warren positions himself behind a couple of passengers, pulling them in front of him.

As the briefcase empties out onto the floor we see a metal film can, comic books, toothbrush, spare undies, condoms, and a small teddy bear tumble out onto the floor in front of him.

NIGEL
Officer you've got the wrong man!

WARREN
(standing, dusting himself off)
We'll decide who the wrong man is you blithering idiot!

CYRIL

Now what's in the tin can and be quick about it.

                NIGEL
                (stalling)

Tin can?

                WARREN
            (threatening, pushing him
              up against the door)

Don't muck us around, Nigel. You've pissed me off enough already.

                CYRIL

Are you fully apprised of the contents of the said can, son?

                NIGEL

Yes, yes, I should think so...

                WARREN

Well ?

                NIGEL

It's...it's...precious undeveloped documentary footage from my study of contemporary royalty.

                CYRIL

Don't give us that eyewash.

                WARREN

Open it.

                NIGEL

I can't.

                CYRIL

Open it.

                NIGEL

I'm warning you...You're about to destroy the only footage in the world of Prince Charles and Lady Di riding the big walrus at SeaWorld.

WARREN
(nodding for him to go forward)
Open it Cyril.

CYRIL
(protesting)
Ah Senior.

WARREN
I'll shout you a Fosters after work.

CYRIL
(resignedly)
Shit.

WARREN
Just follow 'Procedure' and look out for tremblers

DANNY
Look out for knee tremblers, Cyril.
(chuckles)

With excruciating caution Cyril inches his way towards the can of film, gingerly bends down and carefully picks it up and gently twists the lid off.

DANNY
BANG!

Cyril jumps about three feet - much to Danny's amusement. Warren rounds on him.

WARREN
(to Danny)
Right! That's it. You're finished! I'm throwing away the key...

Meanwhile the lid rolls away from the film can, revealing: not undeveloped film so much as a clear plastic bag containing dry, green herbal matter.

CYRIL
(thrilled)
Ah ha!
What have we got here, Senior?

It's enough to draw Warren's attention off Danny.

WARREN
Funny looking film, Nigel?

CYRIL
(beaming)
Must be a Nature documentary, Senior.

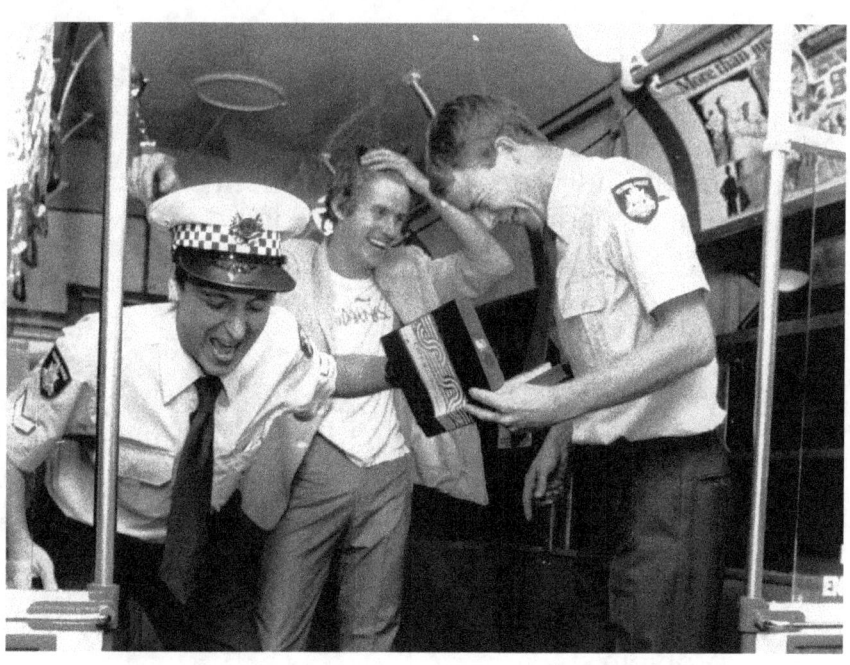

The two cops bend over laughing a their joke.
Obviously relieved that it's not a bomb after all. But a
promotion-enhancing drug bust.

NIGEL
Oh right, right. Sorry, I - must've gotten the cans mixed up. Must've left the doco...at the motel. That's the tin with my colt's foot tea.

Cyril picks up the bag and opens it's snap lock.
Sniffing appreciatively.
Reeling back with exaggerated effect.

CYRIL
Doesn't smell like any part of the horse I recognize, Senior.

WARREN
Bet it gives a bit of a kick, though, eh, Nige...?

Again Warren and Cyril think that's a huge joke and
start slapping their knees in delight. Cathy sighs. Like,
here she goes again...Nigel the walking disaster.

CATHY
I don't believe this.

NIGEL
Look, forgoddsake, I go to a naturopath, you know? I have a bladder infection and consequent ...circulation problems. Colts Foot tea helps thin the blood. It's good for the...
(appealing to her)
Cathy, Cathy, will you tell them about my circulation problem...

WARREN
Don't reckon you'll have any circulation problems for the next few years or so, Nigel.

Again Warren and Cyril think it's the funniest thing they've ever heard.

NIGEL
Officer it's a simple medicinal herb!
(turning to her)
Cathy, at least tell them about my special liver complaint...

But Cathy stares fixedly ahead, completely ignoring him.

NIGEL
It's Colt's Foot Tea!!

WARREN
We have another name for it son: "Cannibal's Saliva".

Laughter. Nigel is desperate.

NIGEL
Cathy will you please...tell them!

Warren finally turns in the direction of Nigel's appeal. Sizes Cathy up.

WARREN
Are you apprised of the suspect's identity, Miss?

Cathy just wishes the ground would swallow her.

NIGEL
(prompting/nodding)
Cathy-

WARREN
Well, Miss?

Cathy takes a deep breath.

CATHY
I've never seen him before in my life.

Nigel is astonished at her betrayal. He starts gasping for air, a panic attack looming. Cyril comes up to uncuff him from the hand rail.

NIGEL
Ah what!!

CYRIL
(leading him away)
Come on, Nige...

As he leads Nigel towards the door, Nigel takes it out on Cathy.

NIGEL
(angry)
Thanks for nothing!

NIGEL(cont.)
(then appealing)
I mean you're not interested in any part of my body are you? What about my bladder, Cathy?

Warren pulls the cord to stop the tram and goes to gather up Danny and Sam, who are still handcuffed together. The following exchanges are all jumbled up with people anxiously talking over each other:

SAM
Could somebody call the *Toorak Times*? And my husband? Michael Hart Byrne - the well known tax evader of 132 Narrak Avenue, North Balwyn. Could some one please tell him his wife's been arrested.
(laughing as she's carried off)

CYRIL
(pocketing Nigel's bag of dope)
Yeah, just tell him we're all down the station having a nice cup of Colt's Foot tea.

Over which Nigel is still appealing back to Cathy. Hanging in the doorway.

NIGEL
Not even a kiss good-bye?

Cathy remains stoically disconnected.

NIGEL
Even Judas managed that much...

Danny is trying to struggle free of Warren's clutches as the three of them step down onto the roadway, stopping traffic. Danny realises he's back where he started. Chucked off again.

DANNY
It's just not bloody fair! I only wanted to go home! I tell ya... It's my right to go where I paid to go!

Danny spots Terry in the tram window, grinning broadly back at him. Pushing his tongue up against the glass.

DANNY
It's that young punk bastard.
(pointing back at him)
He started it. Why doncha arrest him fercrissake.

NIGEL
I can't go to prison, Cathy, I'll be raped!

TERRY
(turning to the passengers around him)
Talk about tickets on himself.

By now Warren, Cyril, Danny, Sam and Nigel are careering across the road towards the footpath, handcuffed together and holding up the traffic like some mad scrum in a rule-challenged rugby game.

Nigel starts actually trying to sit down on the gutter, or at best wrap his legs around a dust bin, or a lamp post, anything to resist being carted off.

Warren is forced to half carry him in a circle round the lamp post, Nigel's legs are attached to the post like the spokes of a wheel:

NIGEL
My bladder Cathy!

SAM
(to Warren and Cyril)
But we're having a party at my place, officers, and you're both invited, you are most welcome to join us for some free champers and little rudie nudie…? We've got a lovely pool…. I think the police do a marvelous job. Don't you? Where would we be without you? Perhaps you've got a favourite charity I could donate to?

DANNY
Him, back there, on On that f*#*ging tram. He just got completely away with it. All I wanted to do was *GO HOME* !!!!

It's about the last thing we hear as the door closes and the tram moves on, leaving the writhing, perambulating scrum behind out on the footpath.

For a few moments peace, in the form of silence at least, seems to settle on the tram as people resume their seats after straining for a final glimpse of the mad fracas unfolding on the footpath, attracting the bewildered interest of passing strangers.

But the peace doesn't last long.

Alice has been slowly rising to the boil at all the turmoil that has descended on her tram and virtually ruined her first night solo as a connie.

She strides straight up to Terry (correctly) identifying him as the root cause of everything that's gone wrong.

ALICE
(pummeling his chest)
Why didn't you say something!!

TERRY
(defensive/deflecting her feather
duster blows as best he can)
What ?

ALICE
Why didn't you tell the cops what really happened?

TERRY
'Cause I don't dob to anyone. Especially the cops.

ALICE
You're pathetic. You know that? You've turned my tram into a shambles. You've ruined my whole first night solo. As soon as Mr. Stanley is found by the authorities I'm history as a connie.

TERRY
They won't understand a word he's saying. You saw how ga ga he was. Anyway I told old coot to shut-up, what more could I do?

ALICE
None of this would have happened without that stupid knife of yours.

TERRY
It was only a toy! Ferchrissake.

ALICE
And look at all the trouble it caused.

TERRY
Well at least the old derro's got a bed for the night. And a toilet. Luxury compared to Beckett Park.

ALICE
Three people are in gaol because of you.

TERRY
(shifting the blame to Cathy)
What about her nerd of a boyfriend. I didn't bring him along.

CATHY
He's not my boyfriend.

TERRY
You could've stuck up for him or somethin'.

CATHY
Why should I?

TERRY
He'll be up for dealin' with a stash like that.

CATHY
Rubbish.

TERRY
Five years minimum, two and a half non-parole...
(turning to another passenger)
Isn't that right?

The innocent stranger nods.

TERRY
See, s/he's been to prison.

240

Laughter at the poor woman/man's expense.

ALICE
That's a bit exaggerated. It was only a small bag.

TERRY
Five years I tell ya. That's what the law says. Five years with hardened criminals. They'll break him in there. Nice soft bloke like that.

CATHY
He'll just make a film about it when he gets out.

TERRY
Pity, your son'll never get to know his normal dad... just the broken ghost of what could've been.

CATHY
Look, you know what I do for a living?
Do you think I want to walk into a police station in my work clothes?

TERRY
(laying it on)
He'll come out a ruined man.

CATHY
He's ruined already.

There's a pause as Cathy takes a deep breath, Terry and Alice wait. Exchange a glance, will she or won't she?

Cathy looks down at the mess that's tumbled out of Nigel's briefcase. She considers it all for a moment before bending down and stuffing the teddy, the porn mags, condoms etc. back into the case.

Then she snaps it closed and notices a piece of paper she missed.

Cathy picks it up, stands and reads the first few lines, snorts derisively.

                    CATHY
    I mean, listen to this. This is what he calls 'poetry'?
                    (reading)
    "Oh Muckdonald's!
    Why am I always looking at your children's
    Playgrounds through barbed wire?
    Sealed off there McDonald Duck,
    Mc Reagan, Mc Donald, Ronald..."
                    (looking up from the paper)
    I mean, he's obsessed, with Donald Duck and Ronald Reagan!
                    (back to reading the poem)
    "You evil puppet Ronald, you shark in clown's clothing,
    Who do you think you are kidding, frozen hamburger?"
                    (appealing to all and sundry)
    I mean, really - I'm supposed to save this!?

                    ALICE
                    (nodding)
    It *is* pretty bad.

                    TERRY
    Doesn't even rhyme.

                    CATHY
                    (reading the final bit)
    "The same old neon restaurant,
    Same old yellow sign,
    Cloned a thousand times over,

Through the brick, mushroom suburbs of the mind..."

ALICE
(commenting/ trying to find the upside)
But sort of deep in a way...

She's quietly encouraging Terry to be more positive. Nudging him forward...

TERRY
What? Oh yeah, it does have a certain ring to it.
Like a ring... you know... hitting the floor of his cell.
His ring- after his finger gets cut off in a card game.

Alice kicks him. He jumps,

TERRY
No... it's real good, love.
They'll soon flog that sort of stuff out of him.
(another hard nudge from Alice)
Could only be an improvement really...
But no, go for it.
Save the poor bugger while you still can.

CATHY
(folding the 'poem' away)
Nigel Davidson, Balmain, 11th November 1975...

ALICE
He needs help alright.

CATHY
Okay okay!

Cathy gathers her stuff together with Nigel's case and pulls the cord to stop the tram.

CATHY

I'm going!
>(resigned)

I'll go back and do what I can. But if they let him out on bail he better be on the first plane back to Sydney in the morning. He can sleep on the couch and maybe see his son for the first time for a few minutes before the taxi.

The tram stops and Cathy heads out into the night, looking for a cab to take her back to the police station.

Terry starts strumming his instrument again. Alice is peering out through the door.

> **TERRY**
> (excited)

Is she going? Is she doing it?

> **ALICE**

Yeah, I think so...

> **TERRY**
> (high fives her)

We did it!

> **ALICE**

Yeah...

But there's a sad edge to Alice. She turns back to a final bit of dusting and cleaning up.
The end of another trip.
Her last.

> **ALICE**

Must be nice to have some one to look after you...

> **TERRY**

I'll look after you...

244

ALICE

You? Look after *me*?

TERRY

Yeah.

ALICE

Fat chance.

But Terry commences to serenade Alice with a final song. A few bars in ... and she starts to respond and eventually comes round.

So that Terry's solo becomes a duet and by the end there's a moment where Terry and Alice are so close their lips tremble on the edge of a kiss.

However, at the last moment she pulls back. He's immediately despondent.

      TERRY
 What?
      ALICE
    (back to reality)
You've cost me my job!

      TERRY
Great, so now you *can* come out with me.

      ALICE
And what about tomorrow. How will I pay the rent?

      TERRY
You can stay at my place.

      ALICE
In your dreams.

TERRY

Wet dreams.

ALICE
(reacting)

That's disgusting.

TERRY

Why not?

ALICE

I've got to take this tram back to the depot.

TERRY

Mind if I come?

ALICE

Yes!

Alice gives up.

At which point the tram finally arrives back at the Mont Albert terminus, from which it started 110 minutes before. As it comes to a halt, the doors open.

ALICE
Good-night everyone.
Hope you had a wonderful trip.
Sorry about the kerfuffle before.
Please don't say anything...
I might still have a job,
Unless they do find Mr. Stanley....

Terry also waves good-bye. Shaking hands.

TERRY
Thanks for coming. Lovely to have you.

As all of the passengers leave...Alice turns back to Terry.

He starts strumming the banjo again, moving into a big serenade.

ALICE
Where do you think you're you going?

TERRY
Thought I might go back to the depot.

ALICE
This tram is closed.

TERRY
Oh goody ....

ALICE
No way Jose...
Get off..

The doors close, locking them both inside, where they go on arguing as the tram pulls out again, heading back to the Hawthorn depot...

The last glimpses of it reveal Alice moving away from Terry, attacking him with her feather duster. He continues to duck and weave while attempting to serenade her with his banjo.

THE END

CRITICAL RECEPTION

1982 saw TheatreWorks bounce back with its marvelous *Storming Mont Albert By Tram*...one of the most original and surreal events ever to animate Melbourne Theatre. It played to packed trams for 14 weeks and has more than confirmed the viability of TheateWorks.
Jack Hibberd *The Age Weekender*

Storming Mont Albert By Tram captured the (community theatre) movement's overall style superbly, a pungent parody set on a moving tram, with a nightly load of passengers as the audience. It played to packed trams for four months.
Rhonda Pelletier and Des Files *Theatre Extra*

Suburban theatre is booming in Melbourne. A new idea...this theatre is a moving tram! The play has had such a tremendous success it is running indefinitely...
Carole Veitch *Melbourne Herald*

Stormtroupers hit the Mont Albert track. Anyone who rides on a tram knows the feeling of being a spectator at a series of tiny individual dramas. Passengers are like theatre audience members, randomly assembled in a confined space for a short period of time, participants in a ritual with potential for the unexpected...The play takes place entirely on the tram, which travels into the city and back to Mont Albert. Each audience member-cum-traveller is issued with a giant sized mock travel card. They climb aboard, take a seat, look around. Very much like a normal tram. Except the conductress introduces herself: "Hi I'm Alice Cronin and this is my very first night." The play has caught the public interest. There are only a few seats left for the reason of the season.
Phillipa Hawker *The Age*

On a Friday evening at approximately 9.20 pm a green tram travelling east along Victoria Parade, Fitzroy narrowly missed colliding with two buses travelling in convoy south along Brunswick Street. Passengers in all vehicles were stunned but sustained no injuries except for a debilitating contortion of the facial muscles... for theatre goers a unique event. Only the drivers were real. Using chartered public transport, the Bus and Tram shows are exploring different relationships between actors and audiences by creating theatrical events in everyday environments...

the usual division between audience and performance is challenged which gives rise to ambiguities that are confronting and often hilariously funny… the shows expose and flout the rules of watching. They give us the right to watch unabashed in situations which we are normally reticent. At other times we are the ones being watched.
Suzanne Spunner *The National Times*

Another clever tram idea, *Storming Mont Albert By Tram* is a chaotic comedy booked out for months.
John Allen and Claude Forrel *Melbourne Living*

(*Storming Mont Albert By Tram*) has great tourist potential. It was phenomenally successful… I can see it becoming something like *The Mousetrap* was in London, a real tourist drawcard.
Don Dunstan (former premier of South Australia) *The Age*

Storming Mont Albert By Tram is a unique theatrical experience based on a series of actual incidents that the writer and cast have collected over lifetimes of travel on public transport. A progression of curious and hilarious incidents that occur as the tram makes its way to the city and back. Relationships develop and fall part. There is humour, pathos and desperation. A documentary play about the nature of Melbourne's trams and the people who use them. The characters are drawn from the suburbs in which they appear to live.
Moomba Festival of Theatre

Paul Davies has got a good deal of mileage from the incidents he witnessed. He also used his experiences in a short story which won a prize in the *Journal's* short story competition.
Phillipa Hawker *The Age*

A unique and intriguing production
Eastern Standard

It's not every day that you can watch a stage play on a moving tram. But that's what Melbourne "commuters" are doing during Moomba this year… If a play in a tram is not a world first, it's certainly very close to it.
TV Scene

Visitors from faster and trendier cities used to say there wasn't much fun at night in Melbourne. But not anymore. This year two hilarious night rides have grabbed the headlines. *Storming Mont Albert By Tram* is a sequence of amusing and startling "happenings". The commuters (audience) were starting to get the hang of the show and loving the diversion. But they weren't sure about the warring couple whose conversation sounded too real to be play-acting. None of it was real, but all of it was the sort of thing that COULD happen.
Laurie Landray *Australasian Post*

Innovative, a bizarre theatrical first: a play on a tram.
Eastern Standard

One of the most memorable moments involved an off-duty policeman who got on the tram unaware that a play was being acted out inside. The play was at the point where a drunken derelict and a conductress are arguing about the drunk's attempts to buy a ticket with a pound note. He approaches the conductress ID in hand and asks if the drunk is giving any trouble. While she was trying to deal with the policeman the derelict was trying to keep the play moving by offering his pound note. The policeman swung round and asked "Oh come on mate, how many times have you tried that one?" The audience loved it. On another occasion the drunk had just been thrown off the stage tram when an ordinary tram squealed to a halt. The driver leapt out, grabbed Danny, put him in a half nelson and called out "I've got him. I've got him!"
Deidre Black *Eastern Standard*

Innovative, valid with elements of street theatre. It involves the eastern suburbs and focuses on an area not noted for avant garde theatre. Any form of innovation is welcome in these dreary days.
John Hindle *Sunday Observer*

Taking Melbourne By Storm! A bizarre but entertaining sequence of events.
METRA (the news vehicle for MMTB employees)

Every tram should have one. Car drivers and prospective passengers along the Mont Albert route into Collins Street have been intrigued by some strange goings on this week. Of course this is not a regular journey but a neat bit of innovation by TheatreWorks. The audience loved it all. One said riding on trams would never be the same again. Another said "Every tram should have a resident drama company."
Laurie Landray *The Melbourne Herald*

Tram Stormed Mont Albert. *Storming Mont Albert By Tram* had a riotous debut on its tram trip from Mont Albert to Melbourne and back last Thursday night.
Progress Press

The funniest things happen on trams. In an attempt to expose the curious, humorous, idiosyncratic folly and genius of the situations which arise while tram trolleying TheateWorks is performing the world's first ever play on a tram. An inspired piece of lunacy. The production has enough scope for improvisation to accommodate the audience as actors. Nobody actually identifies themselves they simply start talking.

A unique repertory conception, a play on a specially hired green tram is a theatre highlight of Melbourne's Moomba festival. The show is built for laughs
Progress Press

Storming Mont Albert By Tram not only takes theatre out to the people it makes theatre out of the everyday environment. Sherrifs and Davies have created a complete event that is more than just being on a tram with a group of actors. The event they have created, like real-life, has a multiplicity of focus and the script is only a part of it; what really is at issue and of interest is the subversion of the boundaries between theatre and life. The tram show has done more for the public transport lobby than Travelcard ever could, and en route created original, genuinely popular theatre.
Suzanne Spunner *Theatre Australia*

Storming Mont Albert By Tram has furnished some indication of the importance of the theatrical upheaval in Melbourne. No play with and audience of 50 can pay its way, but it is unique and precious and must be preserved. Technically it is fascinating to watch the cast trim its ad libbing to the actual time between stops. There is something very special about this project which Melbourne must not let slip out of its communal life. Not only are trams virtually unique to Melbourne, but the possibility of stylizing some of the events that all tram travellers have seen has been realised triumphantly. Television brings a form of drama to where we live; this play brings live theatre into the public space we share, not like street theatre, at which we are passing spectators, but to a defined space of which we have elected to become part for a specified time. Needless to say the incidents which make up the script are very funny. The actors from TheatreWorks are revolutionising theatrical space, by performing a play as though it were real life, in the safety of a moving tram. I can think of no better bridge between the community and its own theatre than the sort of re-enactment of real-life fiascos that make up the stuff of *Storming Mont Albert By Tram*
Ken Healey *The Canberra Times*

A wild, whacky idea which took Mont Albert and the rest of Melbourne by storm. So successful was *Storming Mont Albert By Tram* that a three week experiment turned into a three month engagement that has put TheatreWorks back on the tracks financially.
Kay O'Sullivan *The Sun*

The show must go on! The freewheeling Number 42 tram packed with caricatures of the tram travelling society, an expectant audience is one of the most popular shows playing anywhere in Australia.
Free Press

Storming Mont Albert By Tram had a riotous debut on its tram trip from Mont Albert to Melbourne and back last Thursday night. This unique repertory conception will be a theatre highlight of Moomba. The show itself is built for laughs.
Nunawading Gazette

The Herald

The Herald, Sat., May 29, 1982 — Page 11

Dramatic tales stir the suburb

By CAROL VEITCH

Suburban theatre is booming in Melbourne.

Victoria has more amateur theatre groups than any other state and subsidised community theatre is slowly being recognised as a vital part of local life.

Throughout the year, actors are putting on shows in more and more non-traditional venues.

Amateurs are doing it for the love of the stage and many professionals are choosing not to work for the large established theatre companies in an effort to give people in the suburbs, work relevant to Australian day to day life.

Some professionals, working with small companies relying on grants from local councils and the Ministry of the Arts, choose to receive under-award wages, or defer their pay until times are better.

Some companies that try to set up an alternative to traditional theatre obviously fail, but those that have succeeded have done so because they have had the support of the community and their seemingly tireless actors, writers and directors.

Five graduates of the Victorian College of the Arts founded the Theatre Works company in 1980. It is now running a play on a tram.

"Storming Mont Albert by Tram" looks at the experience of travelling on public transport and the experiences the passengers share.

The tram can hold an audience of only 50 and travels from Mont Albert to the city and back.

The play has had such a tremendous response it is running indefinitely, at a loss.

The small audience cannot provide high enough box office takings to cover the cost of the tram's hire or the actors' wages. At the moment the actors can be given only $20 a performance — not financially viable," says the company's administrator, Martin Foot, who is hoping for sponsorship from companies or the Transport Ministry.

Theatre Works relies on a grant of $30,000 from the Arts Ministry and smaller grants from Camberwell Council, student bodies and other government departments.

Martin earns $10,009 a year and is the most regularly paid of the company's 14 members.

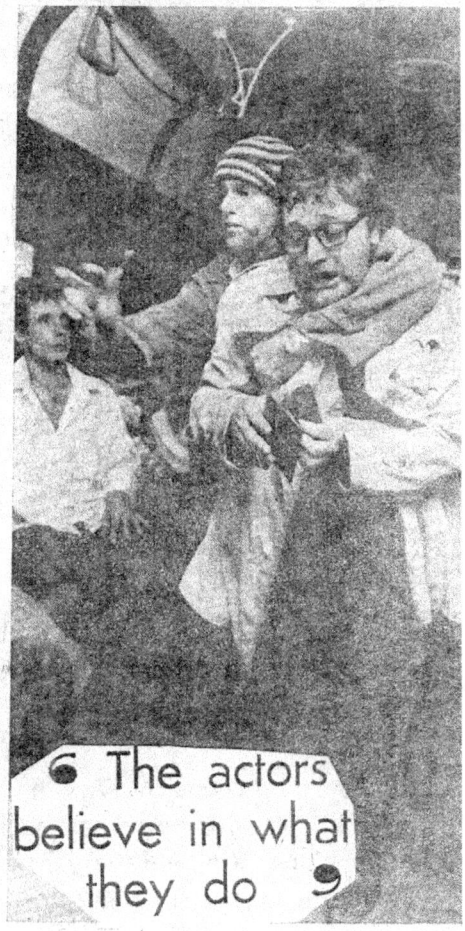

6 The actors believe in what they do 9

A new idea... this theatre is a moving tram.

ARTS REVIEW

Stormtroupers hit Mont Albert track

REPORT
Philippa Hawker

ON the number 42 tram at the Mont Albert terminus, at the corner of Whitehorse and Union roads, a theatrical event starts taking place. Not the traditional location for theatre, out there in the middle of the street, among parked Cortinas and Mazdas, opposite the Combined Family Benefits Centre and the Antique Restaurant.

It is the starting point for 'Storming Mont Albert by Tram', a new production by the community theatre group Theatre Works.

The play takes place entirely on the tram, which travels into the city and back to Mont Albert. There is a 30-minute interval in the Hotel Australia.

Each audience member-cum-traveller is issued with a ticket, a giant size mock travel card with Theatre Works printed on it.

They climb aboard, take a seat, look around. Very much like a normal tram ride. Except that the conductress introduces herself: "Hi, I'm Alice Cronin and this is my very first night." Alice is incredibly bright and enthusiastic, and she is wearing amazing multi-colored shoes that look like toucans.

Alice is going to have a rough night and her troubles begin with the down-at-heel old man with the beanie and the tranny, who turns out to be a former politics lecturer who has fallen on hard times.

Alice also will have to cope with Samantha Hart Byrne, a dizzy socialite who is more used to a Mercedes-Benz than a tram. She is trying to get to the Melbourne Theatre Company production on time, but her row with her husband is uppermost in her mind.

Further along the route we meet Nigel Davidson, a suave young film-maker in a Solidarity T-shirt, who has a dramatic reunion. Then there's the young punk with the lifesize model seeing-eye dog, not to mention the zealous ticket inspector, a failed sleuth with a magnifying glass and a battery of biros in his breast pocket.

He is played by Paul Davies, who wrote the script for the play, based around an incident he saw while travelling on a tram.

Anyone who rides on a tram knows the feeling of being a spectator at a series of tiny individual dramas. Passengers are like theatre audience members, randomly assembled in a confined space for a short period of time, participants in a ritual with potential for the unexpected.

One unforeseen moment arose during dress rehearsal. The production is carefully organised: Paul Davies checked the route with a stopwatch as he prepared his script. The tram makes fewer stops than the regular service and

'Storming Mont Albert by Tram': author Paul Davies as the zealous ticket inspector.

it has "Special" posted on its destination board so that ordinary passengers do not try to board it.

But on the dress rehearsal run, a stocky man in a short-sleeved shirt climbed aboard about half way to the city. It was at a moment when the old man was trying to pay his fare with a one-pound note. As the passengers watched in fascinated silence, the newcomer said to Alice: "Having trouble?" He turned to the old man: "Try this often, do you?"

Director Mark Shirrefs, who was travelling on the tram, unobtrusively defused the situation, explaining quietly to the zealous traveller what was happening. The man turned out to be an off-duty policeman. He decided to stay and watch the play.

There is plenty to watch, to the city and back. The tram's progress even attracts attention from passers-by and car drivers, who cannot quite believe what they are seeing.

One thing becomes clear: a play like this could never be produced on one of the smart new orange trams. They segregate passengers, cut people off from one another. They have none of the feeling of community that the old green trams engender.

Theatre Works is a community-based group, a resource-like public transport, members say. And the tram runs through their local area.

Much of the play was worked out by the group, Paul Davies says. "And early on we took a decision to make the whole thing larger than life," he says.

The project has caught the public interest. There are only a few seats left for the rest of the season, which lasts until Sunday 14 March. An extension or a return season will be considered if a sponsor can be found who will take on the cost of hiring the tram.

● Theatre Works is appealing to the Victorian Government to subsidise its programme 'Storming Mont Albert by Tram' by waiving the charges it must pay to the Tramways Board. Theatre Works must pay, in addition to hire of the tram, the cost of both conductor and driver.

Although the play is an audience success, Theatre Works stands to lose $600 a week during its run — a large amount for a company which has lost more than half its subsidy and faces a precarious year.

Making mirth on the move

Theatre

Storming St Kilda by Tram
by Paul Davies
Theatreworks
Melbourne

HELEN THOMSON

THIS is the second time Theatreworks have set off in a green rattler to entertain the public with a uniquely Melbourne version of travelling theatre. Six years ago they did a show called *Storming Mont Albert by Tram* and they have now come up with a new version as part of Melbourne's Comedy Festival.

If ever you've whiled away the commuting hours musing or fantasising about your fellow travellers' real lives, then this show will be compulsive viewing. Some of the fun comes from the genuine confusion between life and art. If you can drag your attention away from the drama inside, the reactions of passing motorists or genuine travellers trying to board constitute a comedy in themselves.

Paul Davies has written a plot of sorts, but *Storming St Kilda* relies on informality, on pushing beyond the conventions of stage naturalism. There is no escape from the intimacy of public transport, and our private audience space is frequently invaded by actors playing all too familiar roles.

In fact the characterisation consists entirely of stereotypes, with much of the humour arising from the very predictability of their behaviour. Alice the conductor is a battler with a heart of gold, Danny the Derro makes precisely the public nuisance of himself of which drunks have always been capable.

When Cathy and Nigel accidentally meet after parting 14 years earlier and throw the normal inhibitions of public behaviour to the winds, we eavesdrop avidly. The anti-social Terry, complete with manic laugh and lots of black leather, is quite terrifyingly familiar.

As theatre it's all pretty basic and familiar. The second half never does live up to the promise of the first, but it's nevertheless made enjoyable by the tram ride itself and the sense that any tram ride might well contain the possibility of such drama or throw up similarly uninhibited characters and behaviour.

Director Mark Shiffefs has got together an excellent cast who tackle their roles with both conviction and gusto. I particularly liked Jeremy Stanford's Terry, so locked into the reflex responses of the punk we never were sure whether he was sane, drugged or daft.

Peter Finlay deteriorated from yuppie assurance to primal screaming (he has a teddy bear in his briefcase) with his pretensions satisfyingly exploded.

You may not be much edified by *Storming St Kilda by Tram*, but you're bound to enjoy this robust slice of Melbourne life, an entirely appropriate offering for its Comedy Festival.

The Canberra Times

To serve the National City and through it the Nation

Re-enactment of real-life fiascos

THEATRE
By KEN HEALEY

WHEN I enthused a few weeks ago about an extraordinary piece of theatre in Melbourne, 'Bus, Son of Tram', I was not aware quite how advanturous theatre was becoming in the staid city of the south. 'Storming Mont Albert by Tram' has furnished some indication of the importance of the theatrical upheaval.

Writer Paul Davies won a prize earlier this year in an Australia Day short-story competition. His story was based on events he had actually witnessed while travelling on the No 42 tram. Wasting no time, Theatre Works, a new community theatre group working in the eastern suburbs, commissioned Davies to turn his story in to a script in time for Moomba. 'Storming Mont Albert by Tram' was then presented as part of the annual festivities last month.

Such was its success that a return season is now fully booked, and the future of the play depends solely on subsidy from some Melbourne public institution: the Tramways Board, the Tourist Bureau, the City Council, something. It is essential because no play with a cast of eight and an audience of 50 can pay its way. But it is unique and precious, and must be preserved.

The audience boards a No 42 tram at Mont Albert terminus, under the watchful eye of conductress Mary Sitavenos, a gifted comedienne whose devotion to her tram is equalled only by her love of her audience. Other performers board and leave the tram during the journey to town and back to the terminus.

Interval is half an hour at the Hotel Australia; the characters who share the audience's ride ensure that there is never a dull or idle moment on board.

Technically, it is fascinating to watch the cast trim its ad libbing to the actual time between stops. I can imagine that some audiences become far more involved than the largely invited one of which I was part. Debriefing in a cafe at the Mont Albert terminus is an enjoyable, almost integral part of the night's experience.

So much for simple description. There is something very special about this project, which Melbourne must not let slip out of its communal life. Not only are trams virtually unique to Melbourne, but the possibility of stylising some of the events that all tram travellers have seen has been realised triumphantly.

Television brings a form of drama to where we live; this play brings live theatre into the public space we share, not like street theatre, at which we are passing spectators, but to a defined space of which we have elected to become part for a specified time.

Needless to say, the incidents which make up the script of 'Storming Mont Albert by Tram' are very funny. Besides the derelict, the ex-lovers, the punk and the society matron, there are a couple of stage policemen, called to quell a disturbance. This is not, however, risk-taking theatre in the way that Rod Quantock's virtually unscripted invasion of Melbourne street life is risk-taking.

Quantock, a seasoned pro, is stretching the frontiers of theatrical experience in 'Bus, Son of Tram'. The actors from Theatre Works, on the other hand, are simply revolutionising theatrical space, by performing a play as though it were life, in the safety of a moving tram. Excitement did rise among the audience each time some passer-by became unwittingly involved at a tram stop during an entrance or exit of a player.

So Melbourne's two current public-transport shows are remarkably different. I recommend this one especially to groups of people. In fact, if public-sector support makes the project financially viable, it will become de rigeur for tourists to take this tram trip, much as they travel on San Francisco's cable cars. Imagine three or four related but different shows of this type, each one on a tram in a different part of Melbourne. The flavour of each show would be influenced by local character and characteristics. It should be much more than a dream; the initial reality is already among us.

Theatre Works is, of course, more than a company of actors doing a show on a tram. It is struggling to establish itself much as WEST ha done in Moonee Ponds and th Albury-Wodonga project has done All these groups, composed of gradu ates of Peter Oyston's drama cours at the Victoria College of the Art go directly into the community t work. Theatre Works has hit on presentation which has brought into immediate public notice fa beyond its own area of Melbourn I can think of no better bridg between the community and its ow theatre than the sort of re-enactme of real-life fiascos that make up th stuff of 'Storming Mont Albert b Tram'.

RIGHT: The cast: back row, Mary Sitavenos (conductress), left, Mark Shireffs (director), Paul Davies (author); front, Caz Howard (Kathy), Peter Finlay (Nigel), Hannie Rayson (Samantha Hart-Byrne), Tony Kishawi (the punk), Peter Sommerfeld (Danny the Derro). The script comes from events the author actually witnessed while travelling on the No 42.

27 FEB 1982

Tram ride with a difference

By PAUL STEWART

SEASONED tram and train travellers will tell you that some journeys don't pass without a little drama.

It can be overhearing the intimate details of someone's past, watching little old ladies run the gauntlet of trying to get on or off, or any number of things.

A play which deals with these types of incidents on Melbourne's tranport system is "Storming Mont Albert by Tram" which will be performed during Moomba — and on a real moving tram, at that.

Administrator of Theatre Works, which is producing the show, Ms Jill Warne said: "We all had the idea of doing a play on a tram and when group member Paul Davies wrote an award-winning story about one, we took our script from this.

"It is based on an incident he saw on a tram where this drunk got into a bit of an altecation with this Richmond punk.

"The tram driver locked the doors until the police came, and they ended up arre someone not involv all."

The audience b the tram at Mont A terminus, becor passengers and ac plices in a progressi incidents as the makes its way into city.

The characters g at differnt stops in suburbs.

"Storming M Albert by Tram" Theatre Works will tinue until Sun March 14, and ti can be booked at B

DASTARDLY DOINGS ON THE 42 TRAM

"Storming Mont Albert 57 Tram," had a dubious debut on its tram trip from Mont Albert to Melbourne and back last Thursday night.

This unique repertory conception — staging a play as a specially hired green tram carrying an audience of 50 on its winding journey — will be a theatre highlight of Melbourne's Moomba period up to Sunday March 14.

The Theatre Works Company based at Burwood State College designed this novel way of staging a comedy written by Paul Davies and played out while the 46-year-old tram makes it way to Melbourne along route 42.

The show itself is built for laughs — and dress rehearsal night last Thursday produced an expected one too, when an off-duty policeman accidentally boarded the tram when it stopped and immediately grabbed and started to question a cast character wielding a knife.

The policeman joined in the laughter on finding he had bumped into a travelling show.

First half of the play ends when the tram reaches the corner of Collins and Elizabeth Sts, and cast and audience enjoy interval refreshments at the nearby Hotel Australia before boarding the tram again for the second act on the trip back to the Mont Albert terminus.

Theatre Works Eastern Suburbs professional community theatre company was formed at Burwood State College in 1979, and has been on the permanent theatre and workshop circuit since then.

This show for Moomba, with assistance from the Victorian Ministry for the Arts, will be staged every Wednesday to Saturday evening with the tram leaving Mont Albert terminus at 8.17 p.m. There will be matinees on Saturday at 2 p.m. and two on Sundays — 2 p.m. and 5.30 p.m. until Sunday March 14.

Details and tickets from Jill Warne, Theatre Works administrator, on 285-9287.

● Punk (Tony Kishawi) in a scene with conductress Mary Sitarenos.

● PICTURES BY ERIC WATEMAN

● During interval at the Hotel Australia, play director Mark Shirrefs speaks to audience member Ed Rosser of Mt Waverley.

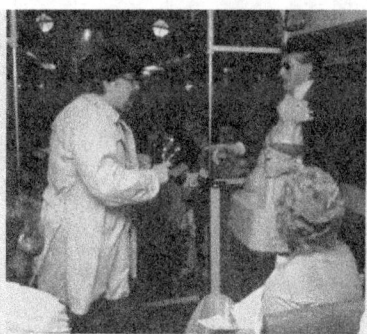

★ ON board the Mont Albert tram — a mobile play that provides a journey full of incident and surprise!

HOLD on to your SEAT..! CONTINUED

exhibits and goodhumoredly suffer the Quantock chaff.

The key to the success of such a tour is its good humor and cool approach, which gets a big test as the party stream into the Sheraton Hotel cocktail lounge just past closing time.

But the presence of 40 Groucho Marxes is a curious experience for the hotel staff. Some of them pretend not to notice this weird burst of potential business, as the false-nosed clientele call for a continental breakfast.

Discreetly observed from afar and askance by the waiters and waitresses, Quantock decides to move, but good fortune strikes at the kerbside when a taxi draws up and disgorges a company of Australia-wide visitors, who wonder what the hell is going on.

Quantock greets them like long-lost family and calls for a welcome from the party.

One of the new arrivals, Des from Western Australia on a business trip says, without thinking: "Come on in and have a drink."

Quantock can't believe his good

had an expense account, which paid for the drinks.

POST took pictures all round, before Luigi whisked them off past Parliament ("the sheltered workshop" said Rod), and the Royal College of Surgeons ("I had a joke about that, but it was cut out").

At the Moomba amusement park it was time for hot doughnuts and a stomach-bending ride on the Pirate Ship and a frantic meander through the Maze of Mirrors — "Get lost and like it".

By now it was past 11 o'clock, and time for supper back at the Banana Lounge to round off the craziest-ever conducted tour of the Queen City of the South.

Meanwhile, in another part of town another 50 happy nightriders are getting over their strange journey to and from Mont Albert.

When they got on the tram it was already occupied by a "derro" who reckoned he was a philosopher, and a hyper-active conductress who thought trams should be installed for

joined by a fancy lady in a Mavis Bramston getup who had missed a taxi and was trying to get to the theatre in Collins Street. She reckoned the derro was just a bit unsavory and edged away.

A trendy guy in dark glasses and red trousers got on at the next stop, and when a few minutes later an uptight dollybird got on, all hell broke loose when they discovered they were estranged husband and wife.

By this time the commuters were starting to get the hang of the show and loving the diversion. But they weren't sure about the warring couple, whose conversation sounded too real to be play-acting.

A carrot-haired punk, boarding the tram with a huge collecting box in the shape of a Guide Dog For the Blind, caused bemused ripples down the tram.

And an inspector, who looked more like a European reffo, provoked a mixture of mirth and sadness as he brought out pictures of his family to gain some sympathy from the punk who was holding a knife at his throat and demanding that he get on his knees and bark like a dog.

The derro somehow got left behind at one stop, but reappeared on the

★ IN Cairns, Don Fry is best known as the go-ahead boss of North Queensland Engineers

Page 18—Eastern Standard, Tuesday, December 7, 1982

Seriously officer, we're only fooling

by DEIRDRE BLACK

REAL life intrusions into the scripted fantasy of 'Storming Mont Albert by Tram' caused more hilarity than writer Paul Davies could have visualised when his play-on-a-tram idea got rolling.

Now, several months after the play's run ended, Paul recalls some of the funnier incidents.

One of the most memorable involved an off-duty policeman who got on the tram unaware that a play was being acted out inside.

The play was at the point where a drunken derelict and the conductress are arguing about the drunk's attempts to buy a ticket with a pound note.

The tram stops, the doors open and enter one unsuspecting off-duty policeman.

He approaches the conductress, ID card in hand, and asks if the drunk is giving any trouble.

While the conductress was trying to deal with the policeman, shaking her head and saying "no, no, no," the derelict was trying to keep the play moving by offering his pound note again.

The off-duty policeman swivelled around and said: "Oh come on mate, how many times have you tried that one?" The audience loved it.

On another trip, the drunk (played by Danny O'Rourke) had just been thrown off the stage-tram when an ordinary tram following squealed to a halt. The driver leapt out and grabbed Danny, put him in a half nelson and called out "I've got him, I've got him."

It seems he expected people from the first tram to assist. Instead, the audience was delighted and some were almost rolling down the aisles in laughter.

Because the play included two policemen, real police often stopped them when they were waiting for the stage-tram to arrive. Police cars with flashing lights were often at the tram stop when the play police boarded the tram. This impressed the audience.

Paul recalls when policemen nearly disrupted the play. The tram was travelling along Victoria St in Richmond when it passed a breathalyser unit. The actors happened to be doing the scene with the red haired punk holding up the tram with a plastic knife.

This could be seen from the road. The police from the breathalyser stopped the tram and were about to board it. Fortunately, the driver was able to stop them and the play could go on.

After that a bulletin was issued to all police warning that the disturbances on the tram were not real.

Paul Davies is now planning another play. He got the idea after one of the actors suggested they should explore Samantha's role.

Paul says he likes to write about people in the eastern suburbs. He has lived in the area for eight years and says he has grown to like the people. For the new play, he thought he would write about Samantha's divorce party.

This will be played on a ferry as it sails the Yarra.

The play, which is not yet named, will have a limited season of five weeks starting during Moomba. Theatre Works actors will be featured, as in 'Storming'.

A PUNK assails his audience, but provokes only laughter.

SAMANTHA the Balwyn trendy

EASTERN STANDARD

HAWTHORN OFFICE
737 GLENFERRIE ROAD, 818 5998

WEDNESDAY, FEBRUARY 6, 1980

HEAD OFFICE 3RD FLOOR DONCASTER SHOPPINGTOWN
848 1214 P.O. BOX 14 DONCASTER 3108

Eastern Standard 23/2/82

Theatrical first

THE assorted company you'll meet on the Mont Albert tram, top row from left: Alice the conductress (Mary Sitarenos), the play's director Mark Shirrefs, the inspector (Paul Davies, the play's author); bottom row, Cathy (Caz Howard); Nigel (Peter Finlay); Samantha (Hannie Rayson), Terry (Tony Kishawi) and Denny (Peter Sommerfield).

THEY'RE storming Mont Albert by tram! Those innovative artists of the Theatre Works professional theatre company have come up with a bizarre theatrical first: a play on a tram.

The audience boards the tram at the Mont Albert terminus and the first act takes place on the trip into Melbourne. Interval is provided at the Australia Hotel, then the second act is played out on the return journey.

The play was adapted from a prize-winning short story by Paul Davies based on an actual incident he observed early last year.

The story revolves around a group of commuters who meet for the first time on a Number 42 tram travelling from Mont Albert to the city. Most of them are looking for a simple night out-on-the-town, but things turn out rather indifferently.

"Storming Mont Albert By Tram", directed by Mark Shirrefs, is presented by Theatre Works as part of the Moomba Festival.

The production will be presented for a strictly limited season, from February 26 to March 14.

Performances will be held at 8.17 p.m. sharp on Wednesdays to Saturdays with Saturday matinees at 2 p.m. and Sunday matinees at 2 p.m. and 5.30 p.m.

For further details and bookings, phone 265 0287.

EASTERN STANDARD

20 APR 1982

● TERRY Meagher (Tony Kishawi) the punk shouts abuse on the 42 tram.

Rolling theatre

THE unique production of "Storming Mont Albert by Tram" is to make a return run due to its recent successes with Melbourne's travelling public.

The show is performed on a moving tram, while travelling to and from the city, with an interlude for refreshments at The Australia Hotel.

Performances will be held from Saturday, April 17, each day except Mondays.

The tram leaves the Mont Albert terminus, cnr. Whitehorse and Union Rds. at precisely 8.17 p.m., except Sunday, when it departs at 5.30 p.m.

This intriguing production is presented by community-based professional theatre group "Theatre Works".

Bookings should be made through BASS agencies.

For further information contact Martin, phone 285 0287.

THEATRE: Laurie Landray

Every tram should have one

CAR drivers and prospective passengers along the Mont Albert route into Collins St. have been intrigued at some strange goings on this week.

Weirdos of several kinds have been seen causing disturbances on passing trams and at stops along the way.

Many a case of the startled double-take has occurred as motorists saw a slightly crazy connie, a derro masquerading as a philosopher, a tipsy Mavis Bramston type, two trendies arguing furiously, a punk rocker with a guide dog collecting box, and a bizarre inspector all at each other's throats.

Along Balwyn way two cops have been seen ejecting troublemakers.

The rest of the passengers in the tram were actually enjoying the scene. They had paid $7.50 for the return ride and a coffee at the Hotel Australia and reckoned they were getting their money's worth.

Of course, this was not a regular journey, but a neat bit of innovation by an eastern suburbs company of professional actors, Theatre Works. Their show was called "Storming Mont Albert By Tram."

The audience on the tram loved it all. One said riding on trams would never be the same again. Another said: "Every tram should have a resident drama company."

Unfortunately, most profits from the production get eaten up in hiring fees charged by the MMTB.

Storming Mont Albert by tram

By Ed Southern

Take a tram and you usually become a player in an unspoken drama of human emotions.

The jerky rattling as the electric carriage bounces back and forth sends most tram patrons into the realms of a uniquely Melbourne state of mind known as Tram Euphoria.

Tram Euphoria causes those blank looks of despair, those drooping heads, flickering eyelids and the look of newspaper fixation. Tram Euphoria is personified in the selfish seat slouch and the primmies who daren't look right or left.

The funniest things happen on trams. The long-lost friend, the argument, the school kids going home, the hitch-hiking dogs, the shopping trolleys, the misplaced umbrellas, the breakfast finishers and late dressers, the drunks and the preachers. It is on a tram that previously unknown persons are wont to inhabit the same space and, accordingly, they each react to the confinement in their own little ways.

In an attempt to expose the curious, humorous, idiosyncratic folly and genius of the situations which arise while tram trolleying, the Burwood-based Theatre Works company is performing the world's first-ever play on a tram (leaving from the Mont Albert depot for the Hotel Australis and back on route 42) called 'Storming Mont Albert By Tram'.

The premiere for this inspired piece of lunacy was 26 February. The 'Free Press' was on board to cover an occasion which should become a future must on the Mont Albert social calendar.

The play IS the people on the tram, and a remarkably clean tram to boot. The Tramways Board, in allowing Theatre Works to play on one of their trams, has offered the spickest and spannest tram we've yet seen. This clean tram was a surprise to the 'Free Press', having been conditioned to grime rather than shine.

The Theatre Works crew — from left, top: Mary Sitarenos, Mark Shireffs, Paul Davies, bottom: Caz Howard, Peter Finlay, Hannie Rayson, Tony Hishawi, Peter Sommerfeld.

The production has enough scope for improvisation to accommodate the audience as actors. Nobody actually identifies themselves — they simply start up talking. If you wish to drop in on a conversation then that's OK. 'Storming Mont Albert By Tram' in the ultimate in transportable theatrical feedback.

"The actors are working with an audience who share the same space, so we're intimate but exaggerated," said Paul Davies, who wrote 'Storming Mont Albert By Tram' from his prizewinning short story first published in the 'Dandenong Journal' (a sister paper of the 'Free Press') as part of the Syme Community Newspapers Australia Day 1982 Short Story Compitition.

"When we lost our funding we though that we might be better able to perform on a tram rather than on a stage," he said.

Theatre Works was almost turned off. After a year of highly successful work the company has received a slap in the face from the Australis Council and all federal funds have been withdrawn. The company is now dependent on a relatively small grant from the Victorian Ministry for the Arts and money raised by public subscription.

The 1982 budget for Theatre Works has been drastically cut. And while the Federal Government is urging arts groups to seek private funding, the Catch-22 for Theatre Works is they haven't got enough time, members and money to lobby private industry for sponsorship.

The company has taken theatre productions to more than 15,000 people in the eastern suburbs in a year and has a commitment to creating plays which "crystallise people's real concerns"

'Storming Mont Albert By Tram' is a tribute to the much-maligned tram. The tram which does not burn petrol, belch pollution or trade itself in after 100,000 kms. Most trams last for more than 50 years.

A variety of caricatures present themselves along route 42, all of which effectively confront the audience.

The Balwyn high society foibled floozie, the Flinders Street station drunkard, the rebellious punk, the neurotic outdated artistically frustrated adman with his briefcase full of rock video clips and trendy ex-wife left with the kids, the conductress in her first night on the job, two uniformed cops, an over-enthused power-mongering Tramways Board inspector, a silent old man and a black dog.

On opening night even Rod "Bus" Quantock, the man who is credited with taking lunacy out from under the theatre restaurant table, made a brief cameo appearance before disappearing into his megaphone.

'Storming Mont Albert By Tram' runs until 14 March. So join in and get along to the Mont Albert tram terminal for a run into the City and back.

Book through Bass or phone 285 0287. If you wish to subscribe to Theatre Works, write to Victoria College, Burwood Campus, 221 Burwood Highway, Burwood, 3125.

The show must go on

The nationally acclaimed "Storming Mont Albert By Tram" theatre production has advance bookings until 9 May after announcing an extended season.

The freewheeling, sparkling clean, number 42 tram packed with caricatures of the tram travelling society, an expectant audience, obligatory Tramways Board staff and a dog who is really a money box first left the Mont Albert Terminus at the corner of Union and Whitehorse Roads on 26 February.

Since then more than 3000 people have taken the trip to the Hotel Australia and back and come to terms with Tram Euphoria, police incursions, domestic arguments, insane tram inspectors and even a substantial dose of fear and loathing in the Burwood based Theatre Works company's show.

So far the extended season will extend until 6 June but because of the way the public response has mushroomed the show might go even longer.

But there is a cruel irony in the success of this unique piece of Luna-Park-Art-Lunacy.

While "Storming Mont Albert by Tram" is one of the most popular shows playing anywhere in Australia, and a great advertisement for community based professional theatre, the theatre works company has been battling dwindling funds since the Theatre Board of the Australia Council withdrew their grant late last year.

And even though the company is enjoying a huge audience turnover with the tram show the circumstances of the staging of the event mean that profit is almost a dirty word.

The small audience capacity of 50 per show and the $115 cost of hiring the tram per weeknight ($134 on weekends) means that the nine actors and production crew have been forced to agree to reduce wages to keep the show on the tracks.

"Our Australia council funding was withdrawn last year because the Theatre Board did not think we had any hope of getting support from other areas," Theatre works organiser and actress Caz Howard told the 'Free Press'.

And yet since the Federal funds were stopped, Theatre Works has managed to raise $15,000 from the Victorian Arts Ministry, $4000 from the Myer Foundation, $1000 from the Students' Representative Council at the Victorian College Burwood Campus and $300 from the Nunawading Arts Council, Ms Howard said.

The Australia Council funding plan for Theatre Works was to have been a three year scheme beginning with a first year sum of $20,000 followed by two diminishing payments during the next two years. However after the initial payment for the first year the funding was withdrawn as part of a Federal Government "phase out" policy for arts funding.

"Even though it was a phase out policy other Victorian theatre groups received small increases," Ms Howard said.

Late in December last year Theatre Work took part in National Stage Crisis Day, when theatres "blacked out" across Australia in protest against funding cuts for the performing arts.

After the protest the Federal Government agreed to allocate $800,000 to the Australian Council of which the Theatre Board received about $130,000.

"We got a bit optimistic, naively so, and resubmitted an application for $42,000 to cover running costs.

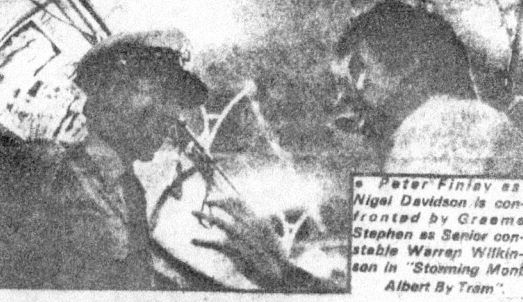

● Peter Finlay as Nigel Davidson is confronted by Graeme Stephen as Senior constable Warren Wilkinson in "Storming Mont Albert By Tram".

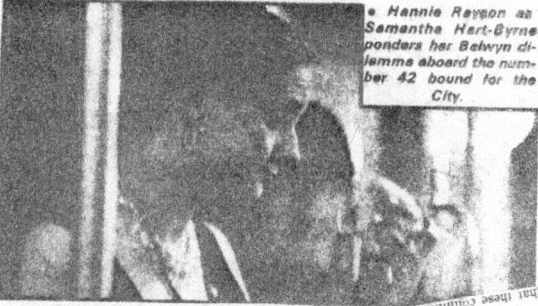

● Hannie Rayson as Samantha Hart-Byrne ponders her Belwyn dilemma aboard the number 42 bound for the City.

"Our total budget was $110,000 and we also submitted other applications for special projects.

"Theatre Board representatives came to Melbourne and held interviews with applicants but we were not issued any invitations.

"So we even had to apply for an interview and we had a talk with them and they said things like 'what will you do if you don't get the money' and things like that.

"Their implication was that our work wasn't up to standard and we were getting a little bit upset about all this," Ms Howard said.

But assistance from the State Government through the Arts Ministry and other donations have enabled Theatre Works to stage "Storming Mont Albert By Tram" and all of Melbourne is better off...

Even though the Big Tram Show is heavily booked seats are still available through BASS.

Theatre Works is also the innovator of a unique series of drama workshops for handicapped children called "Interplay", as well as holding a committment to provide opportunities for Australian writers.

So far the group has been largely unsuccessful with applications to private industry for financial assistance. Patrons have also been few and far between.

Two major projects are planned for later this year and they both depend on a continuing financial base if they are to be staged.

One of the shows is called "MARY" and deals with the problems of growing up as a Greek girl in an Anglo-Saxon Australia.

The show will tour local schools and colleges during October and November leading up to a season at a city theatre in December.

The second is a multi-arts event involving displays, films, workshops and a piece of theatre throughout the winter months "Women of Three Generations" will draw on the experiences and insight of women of all ages to explore changes in women's roles during the twentieth century.

If you can help Theatre Works phone 285 0287 or write to Victoria College, Burwood Campus, 221 Burwood Highway, Burwood, 3125.

THEATRE WORKS

AN INTERVIEW WITH HANNIE RAYSON

JULY/AUGUST PAGE 15

Theatre Works first caught the public's eye with the mobile, 'Storming Mont Albert by Tram' show. Written by Paul Davies in conjunction with Theatre Works, the show was scheduled to run for three weeks. It lasted for four months and drew people from as far off as Canberra.

The Theatre Works Eastern Suburbs Community Theatre Company began in 1979. It was formed by four students from the Victorian College of the Arts. Hannie Rayson, Susie Fraser, Caz Howard Peter Finlay and Peter Sommerfeld, a lecturer at Burwood Teachers College, who suggested that such a company could be formed.

It makes little difference if your philsopy is right when you have no money or no reliable source of funding. Earlier in the year, despite its success with 'Tram', the company was urgently needing funds. Finally the Australia Council Theatre Board gave them special grants of $10,000 for 'Women of Three Generations' and $4,000 for 'Mary'.

Funds for 1983 are not assured. The Australia Council has a policy — The Community/Regional/Amateur Theatre Policy — which contains a 'sunset clause'. The Council undertakes to fund a company for three or five years. In the first year it will meet fifty percent of the costs In the second, forty percent and so on until the end of the period. The company is then expected to rely on funding from private businesses or local governments, and, of course, its box office.

'STORMING MONT ALBERT BY TRAM':
Peter Sommerfeld as Danny O'Rourke (the derelict).

THEATRE EXTRA ·

july

by rhonda pelletier and des files

community theatre:

jack hibberd

Melbourne playwright, Jack Hibberd defines the community theatre movement; "It's professional theatre in a specific area, directly engaging its people and institutions then creating shows and entertainments sensitive to the local history, folklore, recreation habits, work and contemporary issues."

A dry definition, perhaps, but a description of how some remarkably creative people bring unique theatrical experiences to Victorians.

Storming Mont Albert By Tram, performed this year by Theatre Works, captured the movements overall style superbly. Storming, a pungent parody set on a moving tram, with a nightly load of passengers as the audience, played to packed trams for 4 months.

"Along with Rod Quantock's Bus (Son of Tram) it must be one of the most original and surreal events ever to animate Melbourne theatre". Jack Hibberd's public acknowledgement of Theatre Works commitment to community theatre (The Age 'Weekender, 18th June 1982).

Theatre Works, one of several community theatres groups in Victoria is based at the old Burwood Teachers College, part of the recently created Victoria College. Theatre Works home suburbs, or 'specific area' covers Camberwell, Nunawading, Box Hill and Waverley.

Dandenong-Springvale-Oakleigh Journal

Incorporating The Dandenong News

Vol. 121, No. 6 MONDAY 1 FEBRUARY 1982

Portfolio on authors

BRISBANE-born Paul Davies, 32, is a freelance writer.

A play version of his story, Storming Mont Albert by Tram, will be performed by Theatreworks, part of Burwood State College, for Moomba week and the week after.

Mr Davies, of Surrey Hills, got the idea for the story travelling on a tram.

"The general idea of the play is for the audience to meet the tram at the Mont Albert terminus, travel into Melbourne and return," he says.

The idea is a fun night, a series of characters on the tram.

"The audience are more or less passengers. I wrote the story and I'm writing the play. It's an experiment too, of course.

"We're doing it live in the street so to speak.

"There are some advantages and some disadvantages. It took a couple of weeks to write. I mapped out the idea and it took a couple of days to do."

* * *

Mr Jost and Paul Davies, 32,

"SCENE" — 6 MAR 1982, Melbourne, Vic.

NEWS FEATURES

TRAM-LOAD OF LAUGHS

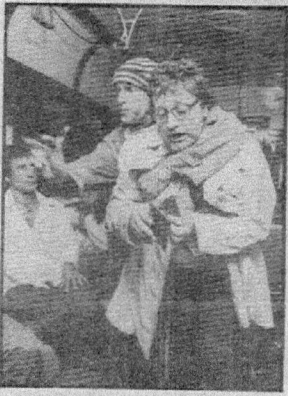

PAUL Davies (a ticket inspector) is grabbed by Dero (Peter Sommerfield).

IT'S not every day that you can watch a stage play on a moving tram.

But that's what Melbourne "commuters" are doing during Moomba this year.

It's the idea of Paul Davies — and the play takes place on a rattling Mont Albert No. 42 tram.

He says trams are an extraordinary form of transport.

"You leap on one and, depending on your luck, sit or stand next to someone who could be anything from an MP to a wharfie," Paul said.

"Then you leap off again."

The play is called Storming Mont Albert By Tram and features a mixture of characters whom you could meet at any time on a tram route.

Actors embark and disembark along the route from Mont Albert to the city.

The tram stops for interval at the corner of Collins and Elizabth Streets.

The tram then returns to Mont Albert for the second half of the performance.

If the play in a tram is not a world first, it's certainly very close to it.

But don't expect to jump on the tram at your local stop, pay a 50 cent fare and expect to see the play.

Bookings have to be made. Each performance is limited to 50 people. Tickets can be purchased at Bass outlets.

Pictures: NEALE DUCKWORTH

ABOVE: The audience moves to the rear of the tram during a "bomb scare".

edited by JOHN ALLIN and CLAUDE FORELL (Epicure)

MELBOURNE LIVING

Rattling through the years

By ROBERT HONYBUN

TRAMS. You either love 'em or hate' em.
Motorists — especially those from New South Wales — curse them with a special loathing.

Commuters have their own whims. They wish they were smoother, quieter, cooler, warmer, faster, slower, cheaper, regular, more regular, less crowded.

Some like them orange, others prefer green. They should be open, they should be enclosed.

But one thing is clear, tourists love our trams. Perhaps this is because they don't have to live with the big electric road hogs. But there are few symbols of Melbourne more distinctive or potent than the humble W class green tram.

Mr Don Dunstan, the director of the Victorian Tourism Commission, also says trams are being used to push Melbourne to tourists. "Naturally enough we feature Melbourne trams as one of the obvious attractions of Melbourne. We found in the United States that with little publicity there the Colonial Tramcar Restaurant was the subject of more inquiries to us than anything else."

Unfortunately, the tram restaurant is still not in full operation because its licence application has not yet been heard. The smart burgundy W class tram with its luxurious interior is now expected to be on the road about a month after its licence is granted.

Another clever tram idea was 'Storming Mont Albert By Tram', a chaotic comedy staged last year by the Theatre Works community theatre company on a moving number 42 tram. The show was booked out for months but eventually closed because Theatre Works were making a loss and wanted to go on with other productions.

Both Mr Dunstan and Mr H craft see great tourist potentia 'Storming Mont Albert'. "I'd lik see it going because it phenomenally successful but fortunately the shortfall in ances for a fairly small group quite a lot and there doesn't se to be another funding source," Dunstan says.

"I can see it becoming so thing like 'The Mousetrap' wa London, a real tourist drawc Perhaps you might have to rev it so that it left from the city, out to Mont Albert and returne Collins Street," Mr Hayc suggests.

Taking Melbourne by Storm

STORMING MONT ALBERT BY TRAM is the title of a popular play currently "running" in Melbourne. It's about people who leap on and off trams, and is actually being staged on a moving tram!

The season originally ran from February 26 to March 14, but has since been extended twice and is now scheduled to close on June 6.

Characters in the play include a charming conductress who loves trams and fervently promotes travel cards, a troublesome but likeable old drunk, a Richmond tough guy with a plastics model guide dog collecting for an impoverished theatre company, young lovers having a "domestic", an over-zealous ticket inspector and an overdressed socialite who normally "takes a cab".

The tram passengers become the audience and witnesses to a bizarre but entertaining sequence of events involving these characters. It all takes place on a chartered No. 42 travelling from the Mont Albert terminus to the city and, with interval and refreshments at the Australia Hotel, back to Mont Albert.

The play is presented by Theatre Works and the tram is operated by a crew from the Kew Depot.

Trams, however, are not the only form of public transport featuring in Melbourne's entertainment life. The Banana Lounge of the Comedy Cafe theatre restaurant has been featuring the sequel to a previously successful play, TRAM. Not surprisingly, this one is called BUS, SON OF TRAM.

After being wined and dined at the Comedy Cafe, patrons are treated to a bus tour to the sights of Melbourne. Highlights include singing Frere Jacques in the Baillieu Library at the University of Melbourne, attending a meeting of the Klu Klux Klan at one of the university colleges, inspecting "typical" Lygon St. terrace houses, and visiting unoccupied suites at the Old Melbourne Inn.

Above: A scene from STORMING MONT ALBERT BY TRAM.
Right: The Comedy Cafe, home of BUS, SON OF TRAM.

Moomba festival of theatre

PERFORMANCE TIMES
- Friday Feb 26: 8.17pm
- Saturday Feb 27: 8.17pm
- Sunday Feb 28: 2pm and 5.30pm
- Wednesday Mar 3 to Saturday Mar 6: 8.17pm
- Sunday Mar 7: 2pm and 5.30pm

Supported by

The Hotel Australia
A Federal Pacific Hotel

storming Mont Albert by tram

EVER caught yourself overhearing some conversation in public and wishing for a pencil or tape recorder to get it all down otherwise nobody will believe it? Worry yourself no longer. Now you can hear it all for real. "Storming Mont Albert By Tram" is a unique theatrical experience based on a series of actual incidents that writer and cast have collected over lifetimes of travel on public transport. The "audience" meet the tram at the Mont Albert terminus (corner Whitehorse and Union Roads) then become passengers and accomplices in a progression of curious and hilarious incidents that occur as the tram makes its way into the city. Characters embark and disembark from the tram along the route. Relationships develop and fall apart. There is humour, pathos and desperation.

After a short refreshment break at the Hotel Australia in the city the tram journeys back to Mont Albert as the second half of the show unfolds.

"Storming Mont Albert By Tram" is a documentary play presented by Theatre Works about the nature of Melbourne's trams and the people who use them. The characters are drawn from the suburbs in which they appear to live as they get on anywhere from Balwyn through Kew and Richmond to the city. Most of them are just going out for a night on the town: to the movies or the theatre or just to have a good time. But it's a night in which nothing really works out the way anyone intended ... join Nigel, Cathy, Len, Terry, Alice, Samantha, Graeme, Brett and Daniel to find out why.

"Storming Mont Albert By Tram" — A Theatre Works Production directed by Mark Shirrefs is made possible by the assistance of the Victorian Ministry for the Arts and through the participation of the Tramways Board and Platform Staff (Drivers and Conductors). Special thanks to Brett Stewart, Graeme Stephen, Simon Dickie, Ken Kimber and Jill Warne (Administrator). Tickets available through all Bass outlets.

Tickets: Adults $7.50. Children, pensioners, students and unemployed $4.60.

The National Times

Australia's national weekly of business and affairs

TIMES REVIEW • TIMES REVIEW • TIMES R

Theatre on the Number 42

ON A FRIDAY evening at approximately 9.20, a green tram travelling east along Victoria Parade, Fitzroy, narrowly missed colliding with two buses travelling in convoy south along Brunswick Street.

Passengers in all vehicles were stunned but sustained no injuries except for a debilitating contortion of the facial muscles.

For commuters an everyday occurrence, but for theatre goers a unique event: all the passengers were participants in the Comedy Cafe's roving theatre restaurant show, Bus, Son of Tram or Theatre Works' Storming Mont Albert By Tram. Only the drivers were real.

Storming Mont Albert by Tram, which opened for a two-week Moomba season, takes place en route between the Mont Albert terminus and the city. Interval is at the Australia Hotel in Collins Street.

It was devised by Theatre Works, a community theatre group which started in Melbourne's eastern suburbs in 1980 in conjunction with writer and filmmaker Paul Davis, who claims to have witnessed the events portrayed in the piece during one memorable ride on the No 42 tram.

Using chartered public transport, the Bus and Tram shows are exploring different relationships between actors and audiences by creating theatrical events in everyday environments.

Their ancestry is in the happenings and events of the late 1960s. Both shows begin with a paying intentional audience and an intentional performance by actors, and acquire a second audience and second layer of performance which is neither intentional nor paying. The interaction between the performers, the bus and tram passengers, and the natives met along the way constantly raises the question, "Who is the audience and who is the show?"

Like Bus, Storming Mont Albert by tram is organised around a tour leader — a zany conductress, played superbly by Mary Sitarenos, and even though it's her first day as connie, the MMTB could not find a more enthusiastic advocate. This woman really loves trams and this tram is her tram. Between stops she dusts and windexes every inch of it while extolling the considerable environmental virtues of tram travel.

The Mont Albert tram makes a number of stops to take on actors playing passengers and at times real passengers are denied the right to board the tram; however, occasionally one does slip through, as on the night I saw the show. It took some time for the audience to decide he was not part of the show.

On another occasion a plain-clothes policeman saw a tram approaching, bearing what looked like passengers running amok. He boarded the tram to investigate; the conductress had a job to convince him that it was "only a show".

In fact the police do make a scheduled appearance on the tram, to break up a fight which has developed among the passengers and on the night I saw it they made an impressive entrance from a police car parked at the tram stop. It was only later that I found out the police car was not part of the show but had stopped to question the actor-policemen about their uniforms.

In Bus and Storming Mont Albert by Tram the usual division between audience and performance is challenged, which gives rise to ambiguities that are confronting and often hilariously funny. If I'm not part of your show then you can be part of mine.

The Bus and Tram shows expose and flout the rules of watching — they give us the right to watch unabashed in situations in which we are normally reticent; at other times we are the ones being watched, even though we may not be doing anything particularly watchable.

— SUZANNE SPUNNER

is its good humor and cool approach, which gets a big test as the party stream into the Sheraton Hotel cocktail lounge just past closing time.

But the presence of 40 Groucho Marxes is a curious experience for the hotel staff. Some of them pretend not to notice this weird burst of potential business, as the false-nosed clientele call for a continental breakfast.

Discreetly observed from afar and askance by the waiters and waitresses, Quantock decides to move, but good fortune strikes at the kerbside when a taxi draws up and disgorges a company of Australia-wide visitors, who wonder what the hell is going on.

Quantock greets them like long-lost family and calls for a welcome from the party.

One of the new arrivals, Des from Western Australia on a business trip says, without thinking: "Come on in and have a drink."

Quantock can't believe his good luck, and the party swarms into the bar for some liquid refreshment. Luckily, Des from Western Australia

POST took pictures all round, before Luigi whisked them off past Parliament ("the sheltered workshop" said Rod), and the Royal College of Surgeons ("I had a joke about that, but it was cut out").

At the Moomba amusement park it was time for hot doughnuts and a stomach-bending ride on the Pirate Ship and a frantic meander through the Maze of Mirrors — "Get lost and like it".

By now it was past 11 o'clock, and time for supper back at the Banana Lounge to round off the craziest-ever conducted tour of the Queen City of the South.

Meanwhile, in another part of town another 50 happy nightriders are getting over their strange journey to and from Mont Albert.

When they got on the tram it was already occupied by a "derro" who reckoned he was a philosopher, and a hyper-active conductress who thought trams should be installed for interstate travel throughout Australia.

The commuting audience were soon

BELOW: The philosophising derelict entertains the travelling audience with a few well-chosen insults.

trousers got on at the next stop, and when a few minutes later an uptight dollybird got on, all hell broke loose when they discovered they were estranged husband and wife.

By this time the commuters were starting to get the hang of the show and loving the diversion. But they weren't sure about the warring couple, whose conversation sounded too real to be play-acting.

A carrot-haired punk, boarding the tram with a huge collecting box in the shape of a Guide Dog For the Blind, caused bemused ripples down the tram.

And an inspector, who looked more like a European refto, provoked a mixture of mirth and sadness as he brought out pictures of his family to gain some sympathy from the punk who was holding a knife at his throat and demanding that he get on his knees and bark like a dog.

The derro somehow got left behind at one stop, but reappeared on the return.

The action and reaction between all these extra "passengers" moved up and down the tram as it trundled its way to and from the city. Some forty minutes after leaving the terminus, there was a half hour break in Collins Street for a coffee or two at the Hotel Australia.

On the return trip the action got hotter, and more dramatic, although it turned out that a "bloodletting" incident, requiring a police call, was after all no more than the derro's squashed pie 'n' sauce. But a few bags of "pot" were discovered in the trendy's baggage, and the cops had a field day.

All in the cause of dramatic comedy entertainment, you understand.

None of it was real, but all of it was the sort of thing that COULD happen.

Theatre Works theatre company love trams, and Mark Shirrefs, the director of *Storming Mont Albert by Tram*, says: "They are an essential part of our inheritance — unique in Australia and the world."

"Every tram journey is a mystical experience ... and everyone has a story of something memorable that's happened to them on a tram."

With this ride in mind, the audience reckoned he was right on line.

★ IN Cairns, Don Fry is best known as the go-ahead boss of **North Queensland Engineers and Agents Pty Ltd.**, the town's **giant-killing firm of ship builders.**

NQEA presently is half-way through its construction program for the Royal Australian Navy's new Fremantle class patrol boats — a contract won against heavy competition in Australia and overseas.

But the latest launching at the busy shipyard caught Don Fry's workforce by surprise. For down the slipway rolled a four-wheel contraption built around a motor bike!

It was the latest mind storm of the managing director, who considers himself as something of an eccentric scientist, forever tinkering in the company's workshops and producing fanciful designs.

His latest effort is, he says, a one-man, four wheel drive amphibious vehicle of quite simple design.

It consists of a lightweight aluminium frame on to which are bolted four, roughly two metre diameter, hollow, aluminium wheels, with paddles welded on to them.

...sed for crazy conductress from the mobile play, *Storming Mont Albert By Tram*.

BELOW: Trundling along the tracks through Melbourne, the conductress confronts a philosophising derelict.

HOLD ON to your S

POST SPECIAL
by LAURIE LANDRAY pictures: BARRY WELLER

★ VISITORS from faster and trendier cities used to say there wasn't much fun at night in Melbourne; but not any more.

These days it's the centre of the theatre restaurant scene where zany comedy acts of all kinds flourish, and become cults.

At Moomba time, when Melbourne's population gives itself over to "getting together and having fun" the comedy splurges into the open air — and this year two hilarious nightrides have grabbed the headlines.

In one of them, called quaintly *Bus Son of Tram*, comedian Rod Quantock takes a busload of diners on a haphazard tour of the town.

And, in *Storming Mont Albert by Tram*, a company of actors called Theatre Works produce a sequence of amusing and startling "happenings" on a return tram ride from suburban Mont Albert to Collins Street.

POST, ever in search of a new Australian experience, went along for the ride with Quantock, who in bushy red beard and straw hat, made his name with rambling monologues about the state of the world and, in particular, Australia.

He organises his nightly tours as a sort of gleeful conspiracy with the customers, who all don false noses and glasses and haven't the faintest notion where they're going.

Quantock himself often isn't certain, and many halts and visits along the way are spur-of-the-moment decisions.

At some of the stops, such as Russell Street police HQ or a hoity toity restaurant, the reception has been decidedly chilly.

After a dinner at the Banana Lounge of the Comedy Cafe, there's a brief "rehearsal" of the party song *Frere Jacques*, which will be sung on the way. Then 40 or 50 revellers board the bus with their leader brandishing a chook on a pole, assisted by his partner Geoff Brooks, dressed in a pseudo Salvo uniform and carrying a koala on a pole.

With Luigi at the wheel, *Bus Son of Tram* trundles up Brunswick Street, Fitzroy, and Quantock decides that a stop-off at the Family Planning Centre is a good idea for starters.

"SSSHH" — he whispers through his loud hailer. "Surprise is the essence of success. Keep the chook in sight at all times."

Up endless stairs, and bubbling with silent excitement, the crowd creeps to a dead end at the top. It is 9.45 p.m., and not surprisingly everything is closed.

"At least we ought to leave a note," says tongue-in-cheek Rod. And spuriously a 'typical Irish couple' leave a message on the door saying that they are going on holiday and need some advice on "planning".

Across the road the Austrian Club catches Rod's eye and he decides to take the party in via a side door, through which music is heard.

"Noses off, and when we're inside, after three whistles, it's into *Frere Jacques*," commands the leader.

Inside a few folk dancers are practising to the music of a squeezebox. As the quiet invasion takes place, looks of consternation spread over their faces. "Who are these people," they wonder, until the tension is dispelled by a chorus of the French song.

Quantock senses how far he can stretch the surprise situation, and calls for a return to the bus "Give us a polka," he asks the accordionist, and the party trips out to the strains of *The Happy Wanderer*.

As the bus moves through the city, Rod's loud hailer dispenses wit and laughter to passengers, passers by, and even a tramload waiting at the traffic lights.

Thrusting his chook on a hook in the tram's direction, he commands the passengers to sing along with *Frere Jacques*, and amazingly some take it up before bus and tram part company.

By this time The Herald Outdoor Art Show is closed for the night, but with a little loud hailing, the party manages to rouse the nightwatch staff, who obligingly display some of the

CONTINUED OVERLEAF

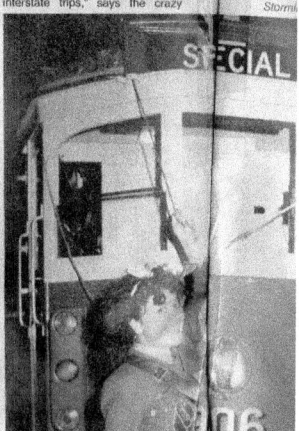

BELOW: "Trams should be used for interstate trips," says the crazy

POST SPECIAL
by LAURIE LANDRAY   pictures: BARRY WELLER

HOLD on to your SEAT..!

★ VISITORS from faster and trendier cities used to say there wasn't much fun at night in Melbourne; but not any more.

These days it's the centre of the theatre restaurant scene where zany comedy acts of all kinds flourish, and become cults.

At Moomba time, when Melbourne's population gives itself over to "getting together and having fun" the comedy splurges into the open air — and this year two hilarious nightrides have grabbed the headlines.

In one of them, called quaintly *Bus Son of Tram*, comedian Rod Quantock takes a busload of diners on a haphazard tour of the town.

And, in *Storming Mont Albert by Tram*, a company of actors called Theatre Works produce a sequence of amusing and startling "happenings" on a return tram ride from suburban Mont Albert to Collins Street.

When they got on the tram it was already occupied by a "derro" who reckoned he was a philosopher, and a hyper-active conductress who thought trams should be installed for interstate travel throughout Australia.

The commuting audience were soon joined by a fancy lady in a Mavis Bramston getup who had missed a taxi and was trying to get to the theatre in Collins Street. She reckoned the derro was just a bit unsavory and edged away.

A trendy guy in dark glasses and red trousers got on at the next stop, and when a few minutes later an uptight dollybird got on, all hell broke loose when they discovered they were estranged husband and wife.

By this time the commuters were starting to get the hang of the show and loving the diversion. But they weren't sure about the warring couple, whose conversation sounded too real to be play-acting.

A carrot-haired punk, boarding the tram with a huge collecting box in the shape of a Guide Dog For the Blind, caused bemused ripples down the tram.

And an inspector, who looked more like a European reffo, provoked a mixture of mirth and sadness as he brought out pictures of his family to gain some sympathy from the punk who was holding a knife at his throat and demanding that he get on his knees and bark like a dog.

The derro somehow got left beh[ind] at one stop, but reappeared on return.

The action and reaction between these extra "passengers" moved and down the tram as it trundled way to and from the city. Some f[or] minutes after leaving the termi[nus] there was a half hour break in Col[lins] Street for a coffee or two at the H[otel] Australia.

On the return trip the action hotter, and more dramatic, althou[gh it] turned out that a "bloodlett[ing]" incident, requiring a police call, after all no more than the de[bris of] squashed pie 'n' sauce. But a few b[ags] of "pot" were discovered in trendy's baggage, and the cops ha[d a] field day.

All in the cause of dram[a and] comedy entertainment, understand.

★ ON board the Mont Albert tram — a mobile play that provides a journey full of incident and surprise

Progress Press

DISTRIBUTED THROUGHOUT CAMBERWELL, HAWTHORN, KEW AND BOX HILL

'Leader in the Community'

Conductress (Mary Sitarenos) and socialite (Hannie Rayson) of Collingwood in action.

This unique repertory conception a play staged on a specially-hired green tram carrying an audience of 50 on its evening journey is a theatre highlight of Melbourne's Moomba period.

It was devised by the Theatre Works Company based at Burwood State College. The comedy written by Paul Davies is played out while the 50 years old hire tram makes its way to Melbourne along Route 42.

The show itself is built for laughs — and dress rehearsal night last Thursday produced an expected one, too, when an off-duty policeman accidentally boarded the tram when it stopped and immediately grabbed and started to question a character wielding a knife.

The policeman joined in the laughter on finding he had bumped into a travelling show.

First half of the play ends when the tram reaches the corner of Collins and Elizabeth St and cast and audience enjoy interval refreshments at the nearby Hotel Australia before boarding the tram again for the second act on the trip back to the Burwood terminus.

Theatre Works Eastern Suburbs professional community theatre company was formed at Burwood State College in 1979 and has been on the permanent theatre and workshop circuit since then.

This show, with assistance from the Victorian Ministry for the Arts, will be staged every Wednesday to Saturday evening with the tram leaving the tram leaving Mont Albert terminus at matinees on Saturday at 2 pm and two on Sundays — 2 pm and 5.30 pm until Sunday March 14.

Details and tickets from Jill Warne, Theatre Works administration on 285 0287.

Pictures by Eric Waterman.

Progress Press
INCORPORATING BOX HILL GAZETTE
Wednesday, February 13, 1980

PROGRESS PRESS, Wednesday, March 3, 1982 — Page 17

The Inspector, played by Paul Davies, of Surrey Hills, has his hands full in this scene. Paul wrote the play.

Tram stormed Mont Albert

"Storming Mont Albert by Tram" had a riotous debut on its tram trip from Mont Albert to Melbourne

Progress Press
Leader in the Community
DISTRIBUTED THROUGHOUT CAMBERWELL, HAWTHORN, KEW AND BOX HILL.

Page 12 — PROGRESS PRESS, Wednesday, February 24, 1982

PLAYERS FEEL THEY'RE "ON THE RIGHT TRAM"

● Cast members in front of their tram theatre.

In its long lifetime, a Melbourne tram could be called many things. But never surely a theatre. Until now.

On Friday, February 26 at 8.17 p.m. sharp, a chartered No. 42 tram from Mont Albert will set off with an unusual cargo of players and audience.

For it will be the venue of the world premiere of a play titled, most appropriately, "Storming Mont Albert by Tram."

(And it would have to be the world first for a tram-car theatre, surely.)

Yes — the whole play is staged in the moving tram. The "Theatre Works" company will present the first act on the way to the Collins St. and Elizabeth St. intersection.

Interval can be spent at the Hotel Australia, and 30 minutes later the audience will re-board the tram for the second act en route to the Mont Albert terminus.

The play has been adapted from the prize-winning short story by Paul Davies, which was based on an actual incident observed by the author last year on the same tram.

It will be presented as part of the Moomba programme for a strictly limited season, from February 26 to March 14, Wednesday to Saturday at 8.17 p.m., with matinees on Saturday at 2 p.m. and Sunday at 2 p.m. and 5.30 p.m.

Ticket enquiries and bookings to Jill at Theatre Works, 285 0287.

Formed by Peter Sommerfield Lecturer in Drama at Burwood State College during 1979, "Theatre Works" is a fully professional company of writers and artists based at the college.

Theatre group wins temporary reprieve

Theatre Works has been saved.

The Burwood-based theatre company which took all of Melbourne by storm with the now famous 'Storming Mont Albert By Tram' production earlier this year has been allocated a $10,000 Special Projects Grant from the Theatre Board of the Australia Council.

Theatre Works has had its back to the proverbial wall since the Australia Council cut all funding late last year. The group managed to survive on a shoestring with assistance from the Victorian Arts Ministry, the Myer Foundation, local councils and student groups.

The new funding arrangements from the Australia Council will only apply for the next Theatre Works production — a variety of community based events centred around women, their relation to society and to each other, called "Women of Three Generations". There is no guarantee of any long-term committment from the Australia Council.

But a spokesman for Theatre Works said the funding committment, while only short-term, was a positive move and gave hope that the group's application under the general funding category in August might be accepted.

"This is fantastic, it's a very positive step," Martin Foot told the 'Free Press'.

"The success of 'Storming Mont Albert By Tram' had a large amount to do with the grant.

"When they originally withdrew our funding they left us to sink or swim and we have swum and that is great," he said.

The new "Women of Three Generations" project has a budget of $19,000. the $9000 current grant will be raised through the box office and from current committments.

Camberwell Council voted $1000 towards the group at its 10 May open meeting.

"Women of Three Generations" is an eight-week community project scheduled from 6 June to 28 July at the Canterbury Neighborhood Centre, Baptist Church Hall, corner Balwyn and Canterbury roads.

Initial contact has already been made with various groups of women in the Canterbury area. The aim is to have women meet together to share experiences and exchange ideas.

There will be writing workshops, discussion groups, lectures, performances, film and drama workshops all exploring the female experience.

"We want to get in touch with ordinary people," Mr Foot said.

"No special skills are needed and we don't want to frighten people off by some high art form.

"It will not be a teachers and students situation," he said.

The project will culminate with a one-month performance drawing on the themes covered by the initial eight weeks of events. A number of part-time workers, professional performers and career people will be contracted for the project.

Women of all ages are invited to contribute to this easy, sharing and creative experience. In fact, that's all you need to participate — your experience. For information phone 285 0287.

THE AGE

The Age, Thursday 25 Feb. 1982   27

SHOW SCENE
by PHILIPPA HAWKER

Getting right away from the subject of haircuts, community theatre group Theatre Works is presenting a rather different kind of playgoing experience.

The work, 'Storming Mont Albert by Tram', takes place on a number 42 tram. It is boarded at the Mont Albert terminus, where the audience become spectators of a series of incidents based on actual events observed by tram-loving playwright Paul Davies.

The first half ends at the Collins and Elizabeth streets intersection, where refreshments provided by the Hotel Australia are available. The second act takes place on the return trip to the Mont Albert terminus.

Paul Davies has got a good deal of mileage from the incidents he witnessed. He also used his tram experiences in a short story which won a prize in a short story competition.

'Storming Mont Albert by Tram' is directed by Mark Shirrefs, one of the founding members of the Murray River Performing Group. It will be taking place on the No. 42 from 26 February to 14 March at 8.17, with matinees on Saturday at 2 pm, and on Sunday at 2 and 5.30 pm. Bookings can be made through BASS.

Sunday Observer

Melbourne, Vic.
-7 MAR 1982

Evolution if ideas

Storming Mont Albert by Tram; Theatre Works — by John Hindle.

THEATRICAL ideas seem to evolve, here in Melbourne as elsewhere.

This show which is staged aboard a green tram is directed by Mark Shirrefs and written by Paul Davies, and it is valid theatre in its own right, even though elements of confrontationalist theatre and street theatre are used.

It is also true that the show recalls work done at the Comedy Cafe: Tram, and Bus — Son of Tram, both used Melbourne transport as a theme, and Rod Quantock still puts his comedy on wheels as he shepherds innocent and unsuspecting members of his audience to various venues around the inner city.

But Storming Mont Albert by Tram involves the outer suburbs, and focuses on an area not noted for avant-garde theatre. What is common to the experience of all urban travellers, however, is the sort of drama that can evolve on a routine trip.

I can well remember an incident that took place on a Number 6 tram some years ago. A pervert was making life miserable for a pretty female commuter, rubbing up against her. A young man helped by separating the two with his own body — but the deviate then turned his attentions on to the young hero!

Paul Davies witnessed an interesting incident on a tram (nothing to do with deviates) and wrote Storming of Mont Albert around it. The show therefore has some kind of validity that separates it from straight confrontationalist theatre, and from the sort of politically motivated street threatre that was seen in the late Sixties and early Seventies.

The show, in which the audience is contained with the players in the confined space of the tram's interior, concerns itself wth the kind of thing that everyone has seen, in one form or another, but the subject matter seems to be somewhat hyperbolic.

However, Storming Mont Albert by Tram is innovative, and any form of innovation is welcome in these dreary days.

27 FEB 1982

Tram ride with a difference

SEASONED tram and train travellers will tell you that some journeys don't pass without a little drama.

It can be overhearing the intimate details of someone's past, watching little old ladies run the gauntlet of trying to get on or off, or any number of things.

A play which deals with these types of incidents on Melbourne's tranport system is "Storming Mont Albert by Tram" which will be performed during Moomba — and on a real moving tram, at that.

Administrator of Theatre Works, which is producing the show, Ms

By PAUL STEWART

Jill Warne said: "We all had the idea of doing a play on a tram and when group member Paul Davies wrote an award-winning story about one, we took our script from this.

"It is based on an incident he saw on a tram where this drunk got into a bit of an altecation with this Richmond punk.

"The tram driver locked the doors until the police came, and then they ended up arresting someone not involved at all."

The audience boards the tram at Mont Albert terminus, becoming passengers and accomplices in a progression of incidents as the tram makes its way into the city.

The characters get on at differnt stops in the suburbs.

"Storming Mont Albert by Tram" by Theatre Works will continue until Sunday March 14, and tickets can be booked at Bass.

TRAM SHOW

by Suzanne Spunner

Outside of the CBD — community theatre is going ahead, with the Murray River Performing Group's production of *Liquid Amber* — Jack Hibberd's sequel to *Dimboola*; an audience participation play set at a Golden Wedding Anniversary party. In the Eastern Suburbs Theatre Works' contribution to Public Transport Theatre; *Storming Mont Albert By Tram*, originally planned to run during the Moomba fortnight, is now into its second extended season.

Like the Comedy Cafe's long-running *Bus* show, *Storming Mont Albert By Tram* takes place outside a theatre; on the No 42 tram running from Mont Albert to the city and back. Both shows not only take theatre out to people; they make theatre out of the everyday environment. Writer Paul Davies and director Mark Shirrefs have created a complete event that is more than just being on a tram with a group of actors.

The event they have created, like real-life, has a multiplicity of focus and the script is only a part of it; what really is at issue and of interest is the subversion of the boundaries between theatre and life. Was that a "real" commuter who got on at that last stop or was it an actor? How do you tell? Is that plain clothes policeman really trying to stop the show — and do I really have to show my ticket to that maniac who says he's the inspector? The *Bus* and *Tram* shows have done more for the public transport lobby than Travelcard ever could, and en route created original, genuinely popular theatre.

*Page 46—The Sun, Wednesday, June 9, 1982

That tram triumph puts 'Women' on the road

IT was a wild, wacky idea which took Mont Albert and the rest of Melbourne by storm.

The concept of using a moving tram as a vehicle for a play was Theatre Works' novel way of taking theatre to (and through) the suburbs.

So successful was "Storming Mont Albert by Tram," a three-week experiment turned into a three-month engagement only finishing on Sunday, that it has put the Eastern Suburbs community theatre group back on the tracks financially.

The interest it inspired is partly responsible for the Australia Council's decision to grant Theatre Works $10,000 for its newest effort "Women of Three Generations," an eight-week project exploring the change in Australian

By KAY O'SULLIVAN

woman and her relationships over the last 100 years.

"Women" is an unusual project for a theatre group. It doesn't really fit into the usual conception of theatre, but that is intentional.

The people behind Theatre Works are working hard to dispel the elitist tag that accompanies this art form in Australia.

The group's administrator, Martin Foot, believes theatre should and could be as popular and dynamic as football.

"But theatre in Australia has never cracked the mass market because of this elitist thing."

One way to break down the barriers is to get the community involved says Martin. "Women of Three Generations" is an attempt to do this.

Women and men are invited to come together and explore the similarities and differences between the generations.

And also the thoughts, hopes, experiences and expectations of those different age groups through a program of plays, performances, lectures, discussion groups, writing workshops and films.

M-LOAD
AUGHS

IT'S not every day that you can watch a stage play on a moving tram.

But that's what Melbourne "commuters" are doing during Moomba this year.

It's the idea of Paul Davies — and the play takes place on a rattling Mont Albert No. 42 tram.

He says trams are an extraordinary form of transport.

"You leap on one and, depending on your luck, sit or stand next to someone who could be anything from an MP to a wharfie," Paul said.

"Then you leap off again."

The play is called Storming Mont Albert By Tram and features a mixture of characters whom you could meet at any time on a tram route.

Actors embark and disembark along the route from Mont Albert to the city.

The tram stops for interval at the corner of Collins and Elizabeth Streets.

The tram then returns to Mont Albert for the second half of the performance.

If the play in a tram is not a world first, it's certainly very close to it.

But don't expect to jump on the tram at your local stop, pay a 50 cent fare and expect to see the play.

Bookings have to be made. Each performance is limited to 50 people. Tickets can be purchased at Bass outlets.

Pictures: NEALE DUCKWORTH

TRAM conductoress Alice (Mary Sitarenos) shows a travel card to Dero (Peter Sommerfield).

...he rear of the tram during a "bomb scare".

...l (Peter Finlay) gets the brush-off from Kathy (Caz Howard).

THE AGE WEEKENDER

Friday 18 June 1982

Nineteen-eighty-two saw Theatre Works bounce back with its marvellous **Storming Mont Albert by Tram**, a parodistic and pungent situation comedy set on a moving tram with a load of passengers as audience. Along with Rod Quantock's **Bus**, it must be one of the most original and surreal events ever to animate Melbourne theatre. Conceived and written by Paul Davies, directed by Mark Shirrefs (a founding director of the MRPG), Storming Mont Albert played to packed trams for 14 weeks and has more than confirmed the viability of Theatre Works.

A fourth Victorian community theatre company, Theatre Works, kicked off in 1981. Differing from other groups in that it is run as a collective, Theatre Works is centred on the eastern suburbs of Melbourne. Its home suburbs are Camberwell, Nunawading, Box Hill and Waverley.

In its own words, 1981 for Theatre Works was a year of piebald successes, due to teething problems and spreading of its gifts rather thinly over a large area. It intends this year to concentrate more on the Camberwell zone.

The Go Anywhere Show, a portable piece for families which had a father character equipped with a metal detector and tent, searching for gold throughout the eastern suburbs, was felt to be the most effective achievement last year along with **Interplay**, a series of drama workshops integrating the intellectually handicapped with normal children. Theatre Works, like WEST and the MRPG, emerged from the drama school of the VCA.

Towards the end of last year the theatre board of the Australian Council decided to cease funding Theatre Works for 1982 on the grounds of the group's alleged lack of viability. Early this year, when the theatre board was granted extra funds by the Federal Government, Theatre Works again failed to attract annual funding, as did the Carlton-based community drama-in-education team, Why Not Theatre.

Peter Sommerfeld as Danny O'Rouke the derilict during Theatre Works' production of 'Storming Mont Albert by Tram.'

Playwright
JACK HIBBERD

Paul Davies is an award winning screenwriter, script editor and playwright who sharpened his quill on over a hundred episodes of Teledrama from classic Crawford series such as *Homicide* (1974-5), *The Box* (1975-76) *The Sullivans* (1976-78) and *Skyways* (1979), to *Rafferty's Rules* (1985), *Blue Heelers* (1997), *Pacific Drive* (1996), *Stingers* (1998-2003), *Something in the Air* (1999-2001) and *Headland* (2005). He also helped spark the site-specific performance revolution in Melbourne in the 1980s with TheatreWorks' production of his first play *Storming Mont Albert By Tram* (1982). What became known as *The Tram Show* played across a dozen years to packed trams in both Melbourne and Adelaide, travelling a total distance that would have taken the show halfway round the world. Its success lead to an outbreak of 'location theatre' in Melbourne throughout the 1980s including three other plays in real places: *Breaking Up In Balwyn* (1983, on a riverboat), *Living Rooms* (1986, in an historic mansion) and *Full House/No Vacancies* (1989, in a boarding house). These works became the subject of his thesis *Really Moving Drama*.

Both *The Tram Show* and *On Shifting Sandshoes* (1988) were awarded AWGIES, along with *Return of The Prodigal* (2000) an episode of *Something In The Air* (ABC). Paul co-wrote the feature *Neil Lynn* with David Baker in 1984, and the docu-fiction *Exits* (1980) with Pat Laughren and Carolyn Howard. His novel, *33 Postcards From Heaven* was published by Gondwana Press in 2005. Numerous articles, reviews, stories and interviews have been published in *Metro, Cinema Papers, Cantrill's Filmnotes, Australasian Drama Studies, Community Theatre In Australia, The Macquarie Companion to the Australian Media* and *Theatre Research International* (Cambridge University). He co-wrote three documentaries with John Hughes (*All That Is Solid, Traps and One Way Street*) as well as *Holy Rollers* with Rosie Jones. Paul has also given courses in literature and creative writing at various colleges and universities including: Southern Cross, James Cook and Melbourne State.

www.ingramcontent.com/pod-product-compliance
Lightning Source LLC
Chambersburg PA
CBHW071859290426
44110CB00013B/1211